# *LORE*

*Capturing Traditional Environmental*

*Knowledge*

Our culture is something that surrounds us, something that is part of us, and is inextricably linked with the land upon which we have lived for thousands of years. Our culture has a past, and it is that past — especially as we find it embodied in our elders — that we are pledged to preserve. It also has a present — a present that threatens our culture, which we are pledged to protect. Our culture lives, and must have a future. We are pledged to promote our culture, especially among our young people, to ensure that they will identify themselves as Dene, in the full meaning of the term. The mission of the Dene Cultural Institute is to work with the people of the Dene Nation, and with other institutions and organizations, to preserve, protect, and promote the Dene culture, languages, spirituality, heritage, traditions, and customs.

IDRC

CANADA

The International Development Research Centre is a public corporation created by the Parliament of Canada in 1970 to support technical and policy research designed to adapt science and technology to the needs of developing countries. The Centre's five program sectors are Environment and Natural Resources, Social Sciences, Health Sciences, Information Sciences and Systems, and Corporate Affairs and Initiatives. The Centre's funds are provided by the Parliament of Canada; IDRC's policies, however, are set by an international Board of Governors. The Centre's headquarters are in Ottawa, Canada. Regional offices are located in Africa, Asia, Latin America, and the Middle East.

# *LORE*

## *Capturing Traditional Environmental*

## *Knowledge*

Edited by
Martha Johnson

DENE CULTURAL INSTITUTE
&
INTERNATIONAL DEVELOPMENT
RESEARCH CENTRE

Johnson, M.
Dene Cultural Institute, Hay River, NWT, CA

  Lore : capturing traditional environmental knowledge. Ottawa, Ont.,
IDRC, 1992. x + 190 p. : ill.

  /Ecology/, /environmental management/, /resources management/,
/environmental education/, /indigenous population/, /traditional
culture/, /folklore/, /social research/, /documentation/, /data collecting/,
/information exchange / — /case studies/, /Canada/, /Oceania/, /Sahel/,
/Thailand/, /conference reports/, bibliographies.

UDC: 574:303.2(=1-81)                    ISBN 0-88936-644-6

# Foreword

In recent years, the value of the traditional knowledge of indigenous peoples, and particularly their traditional environmental knowledge, has been recognized. This has unleashed a flood of research. Some of the research has been undertaken by scientists working alone, but the most innovative responses to this trend have been developed by indigenous researchers working in collaboration with Western scientists. They recognized early on that the main objective was not simply to collect reels of audio or video tape as a form of folklore, but to catalogue this information so that it could be compared from one region and one culture to other regions and other cultures, and, even more, so that it could be brought to bear on policies for sustainable development in remote and typically fragile ecosystems.

This book presents the results of a workshop on the documentation and application of traditional environmental knowledge through community-based research. Organized and hosted by the Dene Cultural Institute (DCI) based in Fort Hay, Northwest Territories, Canada, and supported by Canada's International Development Research Centre (IDRC), the workshop brought together a small number of teams, each composed of indigenous and nonindigenous researchers from Northern Canada, Europe, Africa, Southeast Asia, the South Pacific, and South America. Their primary goal was to discuss effective methods for documenting the unique environmental knowledge and understanding that characterizes the heritage of all indigenous peoples around the world.

In many ways, the workshop was unique. It represented an important initiative on the part of a Canadian aboriginal organization (DCI) and a Canadian development agency (IDRC) working together toward a common goal. The workshop was held in a traditional Dene camp along the shores of the Deh Cho (Mackenzie River) in the Canadian North. Participants flew to Canada from around the globe. Upon arrival in Canada, they faced another extended flight to Yellowknife in the Northwest Territories. From there, they were taken by bush plane and boat to the Dene camp. Daily life and workshop sessions took place in tents, which both represented typical living conditions during actual collection of indigenous knowledge and, unhappily but typically for the North, provided protection from the cold and rainy "summer" weather.

This book examines the process of collecting traditional environmental knowledge while using a "participatory action" or "community-based" approach. It looks at the problems associated with documenting traditional knowledge — problems that are shared by researchers around the world — and it explores some of the means by which traditional knowledge can be integrated with Western science to improve methods of natural resource management.

We hope that this book will assist others to develop effective, culturally appropriate research methods at a time when alternative understandings and approaches to sustainable development are increasingly critical to the survival of our planet.

Joanne Barnaby  David B. Brooks
*Executive Director*  *Director*
*Dene Cultural Institute*  *Environment and Technology Program*
*International Development Research Centre*

# Acknowledgments

The Fort Good Hope workshop was a unique event and many people and agencies contributed to its success. The community of Fort Good Hope put on a show of hospitality that left our international guests with a true taste of traditional and modern Dene culture. The Chief and Council of Fort Good Hope provided generous logistical support for the camp. Star Tech Ltd lent tents and other camping gear and Northern Stores Ltd donated groceries. Special thanks go to Alfred Masazumi, Michael Lafferty, and Joe Cotchilly. They ensured that the camp ran smoothly despite inclement weather and a last minute change of site. Bella T'seleie and Judy Lafferty assisted in setting up the camp, and Mary Barnaby and Margaret Kelly prepared some memorable meals of traditional Dene cuisine. Wilma Schreder of the Dene Cultural Institute made all of the travel arrangements.

Dr Evelyn Pinkerton served as the rapporteur for the workshop. Her work on the discussion summaries and her thoughtful insight on earlier drafts of the introductory papers were much appreciated.

Our special gratitude goes to Robert Ruttan, project biologist for the Dene Traditional Environmental Knowledge Pilot Project. His calm and sense of humour in overseeing the entire organization of the camp made the workshop the success that it was.

Thanks are also owed to the Canadian Broadcasting Corporation (CBC) and the Yellowknife *Press Independent*. Their generous publicity created better public awareness of the value of traditional environmental knowledge and the research that is being conducted to preserve and apply it today.

Finally, thanks go to all of the elders, community researchers, and scientists who travelled from the nearby community of Fort Good Hope and from the far corners of the globe to participate in this unique event. Their willingness to overlook the bad weather and the mosquitoes, and to share their knowledge and culture in the traditional setting that was the Fort Good Hope camp represented the true spirit of international and cross-cultural cooperation.

**Martha Johnson**
*Research Director*
*Dene Cultural Institute*

# Contents

❧ **Introduction**   1

Research on Traditional Environmental Knowledge:
Its Development and Its Role   3

The Workshop: Purpose and Results   23

❧ **Canada's North**   33

Traditional Environmental Knowledge of the Dene:
A Pilot Project   35

Reindeer Management in Canada's Belcher Islands:
Documenting and Using Traditional Environmental
Knowledge   69

❧ **The South Pacific**   89

Traditional Environmental Knowledge from the Marovo
Area of the Solomon Islands   91

❧ **The African Sahel**   111

Documenting Oral History in the African Sahel   113

An Experience in Oral History:
One Researcher's Account   136

&#x1f54a; **Northern Thailand**    141

    Regional Development in Northern Thailand: Its Impact
on Highlanders    143

    Documenting and Applying Traditional Environmental
Knowledge in Northern Thailand    164

&#x1f54a; **Appendix**    175

    A Summary of Workshop Discussions    177

≈

# INTRODUCTION

*The workshop focused on the development of methods to document traditional environmental knowledge for the purpose of local resource management and education. As a preamble to the case studies, the Research Director of the Dene Cultural Institute, Martha Johnson, provides some background to this theme and summarizes the purpose and results of the workshop.*

# Research on Traditional Environmental Knowledge: Its Development and Its Role

## What is Traditional Environmental Knowledge?

For thousands of years, aboriginal peoples around the world have used knowledge of their local environment to sustain themselves and to maintain their cultural identity. Only in the past decade, however, has this knowledge been recognized by the Western scientific community as a valuable source of ecological information. Today, a growing body of literature attests not only to the presence of a vast reservoir of information regarding plant and animal behaviour but also to the existence of effective indigenous strategies for ensuring the sustainable use of local natural resources.

This knowledge is variously labeled as folk ecology, ethno-ecology, traditional environmental or ecological knowledge, indigenous knowledge, customary law, and knowledge of the land. Traditional environmental or ecological knowledge is probably the most common term; however, there remains no universally

By Martha Johnson, Dene Cultural Institute, Yellowknife, NWT, Canada.

accepted definition of the concept. As a field of study, traditional environmental knowledge is much more comprehensive than either conventional anthropology or ecology. Berkes (1992) points out that the use of the term "traditional" is ambiguous and raises questions regarding the cultural dynamics of such knowledge systems.

> In the dictionary sense, "traditional" usually refers to cultural continuity transmitted in the form of social attitudes, beliefs, principles and conventions of behaviour and practice derived from historical experience. However, societies change through time, constantly adopting new practices and technologies, making it difficult to define just how much and what kind of change would affect the labelling of a practice as "traditional."

For this reason, some scholars prefer the term "indigenous ecological knowledge." This helps avoid the debate about tradition and explicitly emphasizes indigenous people. However, similar knowledge is found among nonindigenous groups such as outport fishermen and farmers. These groups have also acquired their knowledge and skills through hands-on experience living in close contact with their environment

Traditional environmental knowledge, or TEK, can generally be defined as a body of knowledge built up by a group of people through generations of living in close contact with nature. It includes a system of classification, a set of empirical observations about the local environment, and a system of self-management that governs resource use. The quantity and quality of traditional environmental knowledge varies among community members, depending upon gender, age, social status, intellectual capability, and profession (hunter, spiritual leader, healer, etc.). With its roots firmly in the past, traditional environmental knowledge is both cumulative and dynamic, building upon the experience of earlier generations and adapting to the new technological and socioeconomic changes of the present.

# The History of TEK Research

The systematic investigation of traditional environmental knowledge began with a series of studies on the terminologies that people of different cultures use to classify objects in their natural and social environments. These early studies by anthropologists and natural scientists revealed that all cultures recognize natural classes of animals and plants, and that traditional cultures are as concerned with classifying their world as are Western scientists (Bulmer 1970; Berlin 1973; Hunn 1975). Much of this knowledge appeared to be clearly esoteric: many of the named species served no obvious useful purpose. Also, there was often a close correspondence between scientific taxa and the categories of plants and animals established by aboriginal peoples (Snyder 1957; Irving 1960; Diamond 1966; Bulmer 1970; Berlin 1973; Hunn 1975; Johnson 1987).

Early studies by anthropologists and natural scientists also recorded indigenous knowledge of plant and animal behaviour. Local interpretations of natural phenomena were often at odds with scientific explanations (possibly rooted in a spiritual ideology); nevertheless, they revealed a wealth of underlying empirical knowledge (Feit 1973, 1986, 1988; Nelson 1983; Berkes 1988; Jones and Konner 1989; Nakashima 1990).

Concurrent with these early studies was a rising political pressure to recognize the rights of aboriginal peoples and a growing environmental movement searching for alternative approaches to Western science and technology. This changing social and political climate resulted in a shift away from theoretical studies to more applied research. Recent emphasis has been on understanding the ecologically sound practices that contribute to sustainable resource use among indigenous peoples and ways that this knowledge can be successfully integrated with the scientific resource management of the West (Brody 1981; Berkes 1988; Feit 1988; Gunn et al. 1988; Johannes et al. 1991).

Traditional environmental knowledge gained international recognition through such documents as the *World Conservation
Strategy* (IUCN et al. 1980) and *Our Common Future* (WCED
1987). Both reports emphasized the need to use directly the
environmental expertise of local people in managing natural
resources. They stressed that sustainable management of natural
resources could only be achieved by developing a science based
on the priorities of local people and creating a technological base
that blends both traditional and modern approaches to solving
problems.

Increased appreciation of TEK has produced a burgeoning field
of research. At the forefront of this research are aboriginal peoples. They are demanding primary involvement in the direction
of TEK research. "Participatory community" or "action" research
has become the accepted approach in studying traditional environmental knowledge. In such an approach, the host aboriginal
community participates directly in designing and implementing
the project, community members are trained in research methods
and administration, and the community retains control over the
research results.

## Comparing TEK and Western Science

Traditional environmental knowledge is generated, recorded,
and transmitted differently than Western scientific knowledge.
The following list, compiled and adapted from several works on
the subject (such as Usher 1986; Osherenko 1988; Johnson and
Ruttan 1991; Berkes 1992; Wolfe et al. 1992), outlines some of
these differences. These statements are generalizations. The different modes of thinking, transmitting, and expressing knowledge are not mutually exclusive for either system. Dominance of
one mode within a cultural group does not prevent many individuals in that same group from being highly functional in
another mode. Social change is occurring within Western society

and among aboriginal cultures such that new values and ways of thinking are emerging for both.

📌 TEK is recorded and transmitted through oral tradition (often through stories); Western science employs the written word.

📌 TEK is learned through observation and hands-on experience; Western science is taught and learned in a situation usually abstracted from the applied context.

📌 TEK is based on the understanding that the elements of matter (earth, air, fire, and water), which are classified as inanimate, also have a life force. All parts of the natural world — plant, animal, and inanimate element — are therefore infused with spirit.

📌 TEK does not view human life as superior to other animate and inanimate elements: all life-forms have kinship and are interdependent. Unlike Western science, humans are not given the inherent right to control and exploit nature for their own interests at the expense of other life-forms.

📌 TEK is holistic; Western science is reductionist. Western science deliberately breaks down data into smaller elements to understand whole and complex phenomena. For TEK, all elements of matter are viewed as interconnected and cannot be understood in isolation.

📌 TEK is intuitive in its mode of thinking; Western science is analytical. Intuitive thought emphasizes emotional involvement and subjective certainty of understanding. Analytical thought emphasizes abstract reasoning and the need to separate oneself from that being observed and to learn about it through various replicable measurements.

📌 TEK is mainly qualitative; Western science is mainly quantitative. In TEK, detailed qualitative knowledge about wildlife is gained through ongoing intimate contact with the resource. Aboriginal harvesters are more concerned with trends, such as whether a population is increasing or decreasing, than with actual numbers. The indigenous system makes population predictions based on detailed behavioural observations and the principle of harvesting at a level in accordance with individual and community needs. Western scientists gather quantitative information to build mathematical models of population dynamics. The models are then used to calculate sustainable yields for the resource. The yields are then recommended for implementation to decision-makers as wildlife harvest regulations.

🖎 TEK is based on data generated by resource users. As such, it is more inclusive than Western science, which is collected by a specialized group of researchers who tend to be more selective and deliberate in the accumulation of facts.

🖎 TEK is based on diachronic data (long time series of information on one locality); Western science is largely based on synchronic data (short time series over a large area).

🖎 TEK is rooted in a social context that sees the world in terms of social and spiritual relations between all life-forms. Relations are based on reciprocity and obligations toward both community members and other life-forms and communal resource-management institutions are based on shared knowledge and meaning. Western science is hierarchically organized and vertically compartmentalized. Managers become distinct from harvesters; authority becomes centralized and flows from the top down. The environment is reduced to conceptually discrete components that are managed separately.

🖎 TEK explanations of environmental phenomena are often spiritual and based on cumulative, collective experience. It is checked, validated, and revised daily and seasonally through the annual cycle of activities. In direct contrast, Western science employs methods of generating, testing, and verifying hypotheses and establishes theories and general laws as its explanatory basis.

There are exceptions to these generalizations. For example, Feit's (1986) work with subarctic beaver trappers indicates that TEK can be (or appear to be) quantitative (Berkes 1992). Also, Berkes (1977) showed that the Cree fishermen of the subarctic are perfectly capable of carrying out controlled field experiments. In terms of recording and transmitting the traditionally oral knowledge, aboriginal researchers are now experimenting with the use of film and the written word.

Western scientists are largely skeptical of TEK. Much of this skepticism stems from the belief that, although TEK may have been impressive in its earlier forms, it is being irreversibly eroded by the assimilation of aboriginal peoples into Western culture and by the failure of elders to pass on the traditional knowledge to younger generations. Undoubtedly, some erosion of TEK has occurred. However, both social scientists and aboriginal peoples confirm the continued vitality of traditional cultures and note that TEK is evolving, not dying (Osherenko 1988).

By the same token, critics often ignore the significant changes that are occurring within Western science. Over the past 20 years, the fundamental tenets of Western science — rational analytical thinking, objectivity, reductionism, and the Judeo-Christian ethic of human domination over nature — have been challenged for being ethnocentric, antiecological, and ignorant of the cultural dimension of technological development. As a result, Western science is becoming increasingly interdisciplinary in response to today's globally interconnected world, in which biological, psychological, and social phenomena are recognized as belonging to interdependent systems (Capra 1982). The contemporary ecological movement — particularly deep ecology, ecofeminism, bioregionalism, Lovelock's "Gaia hypothesis," and the concept of sustainable development — finds many parallels with TEK (Booth and Jacobs 1990; Johnson and Ruttan 1991; Wolfe et al. 1992).

Neither TEK nor Western science should be judged for its worth according to a rigid set of generalizations or a static image of the past. For, as Howes and Chambers point out (quoted in Mulvihill 1988, p. 12), the knowledge system of any culture is constantly changing through the "assimilation of 'outside' knowledge and synthesis and hybridization with existing knowledge." Ultimately, both approaches have their strengths and limitations in solving environmental problems and both are now inseparably interlinked (Johnson and Ruttan 1991).

# Integrating TEK and Western Science

Most scientists, governments, and aboriginal peoples agree that, given the pluralistic nature of modern society and the ecological interdependence among nations, TEK and Western science must be integrated. Despite much discussion on the need to integrate the two systems and a few attempts to establish comanagement institutions, however, the effective use of TEK in decision-making has yet to be fully tested.

Why are TEK and Western science so difficult to integrate? First, there is the urgent problem of the disappearance of TEK and the lack of resources to document it before it is lost. Second, there are the practical problems of trying to reconcile two very different world views and trying to translate ideas and concepts from one culture into another. Third, there is an attitude problem. Cultural barriers and misunderstandings prevent both Western scientists and aboriginal peoples from acknowledging the value of each other's knowledge system. Among Western scientists, the problem of attitude is extended to include disagreements between social and natural scientists regarding appropriate methods to document and integrate TEK. Finally, the integration of TEK and Western science is clearly linked to the question of political power. Under the majority of existing state systems of resource management, TEK is usually subordinate to Western science.

## *Documenting TEK*

The first and most urgent problem associated with integration is the rapid disappearance of TEK with the passing of elders. Orally based knowledge systems lost in this way cannot be retrieved. It is only through documentation that the usefulness of TEK can become apparent and an improved understanding can be gained of the practices and conditions that lead to the breakdown and reestablishment of TEK management systems. For example, what does TEK have to say about the use of modern technology for harvesting? What can it tell us about the allocation of resources and commercial incentives in the current sociopolitical context? How would traditional institutions of authority operate and enforce traditional laws in a modern context? If TEK is to be revitalized, research must be initiated by aboriginal peoples themselves. The guidance of the elders and the cooperation of the youth are needed to make TEK relevant again.

One of the problems experienced by TEK researchers is that funding agencies often require concrete examples of how the information gathered will be applied. It is difficult to obtain funds to gather data solely for the purpose of preservation. Further, participatory action approaches to TEK research, which involve training local people to carry out the work themselves, are lengthy and expensive. Of the studies that have been conducted, most have tended to concentrate on a specific topic, such as harvesting or the ecological knowledge of one species. Consequently, a broad overview of the range of environmental knowledge available among aboriginal peoples has not been well documented.

For many aboriginal peoples, however, TEK is at the heart of their cultural identity and remains a viable aspect of their way of life. For the rest of the world, apart from the ethical imperative of preserving cultural diversity, TEK is important for many tangible and practical reasons (IUCN 1986, cited in Berkes 1992).

**ᴥ** *New biological and ecological insight:* Fresh insight can be derived from perceptive investigations of traditional environmental knowledge systems.

**ᴥ** *Resource management:* Much traditional knowledge is relevant for contemporary natural resource management in areas such as wetlands, tropical moist forests, circumpolar regions, and dryland, high-altitude, and coastal areas.

**ᴥ** *Protected areas and conservation education:* The "protected area" concept may be promoted to allow resident communities to continue their traditional lifestyles, with the benefits of conservation accruing to them. Traditional knowledge may be used for conservation education, especially where the local community benefits from the protected area.

**ᴥ** *Development planning:* The use of traditional knowledge may benefit development agencies in providing more realistic evaluations of production systems, natural resources, and the environment.

**ᴥ** *Environmental assessment:* The time-tested and in-depth knowledge of indigenous peoples about their habitat is a valuable resource in assessing the social and environmental impacts of proposed development projects.

## Reconciling World Views

The second problem of integration is that of reconciling two profoundly different world views. Western science and TEK are generated and validated according to a different set of assumptions.

Western science has the following fundamental assumptions (Wolfe et al. 1992):

**ᴥ** *Reductionism:* the understanding of complex phenomena by breaking down data and reassembling it in different ways;

🍂 *Objectivism:* the belief that the observer must deliberately separate oneself from that being observed; and

🍂 *Positivism:* the belief that what is measurable is scientifically real and what is scientifically real is measurable.

Scientists are often reluctant to accept TEK as valid because of its spiritual base, which they may regard as superstitious and fatalistic. What they often fail to recognize is that spiritual explanations often conceal functional ecological concerns and conservation strategies. Further, the spiritual aspect does not necessarily detract from the aboriginal harvester's ability to make appropriate decisions about the wise use of resources. It merely indicates that the system exists within an entirely different cultural experience and set of values, one that paints no more and no less valid a picture of reality than the one that provides its own frame of reference (Johnson and Ruttan 1991). The spiritual acquisition and explanation of TEK is a fundamental component and must be promoted if the knowledge system is to survive.

Western science also judges the intellectual achievements of its members according to a rigidly defined set of institutions. As Nakashima (1990, p. 23) points out,

> University degrees, journal publications and conference presentations are the milestones which mark the narrow "path to knowledge." Guided by these inflexible norms, environmental scientists reject the TEK of Native hunters as anecdotal, non-quantitative and amethodical.

Even among those scientists who do acknowledge the existence of TEK, they generally apply scientific categories and methods to collect, verify, and validate it. As described by Wolfe et al. (1992, p. 5),

> They seek to recognise their categorizations in native systems, and apply their typologies to what they think indigenous knowledge systems are. Few western scholars are able to accept indigenous knowledge as valid in and of itself.

Too often, information is translated directly into English without examining whether or not the scientific terminology accurately reflects the indigenous concepts being described. Scientific terminology may not be able to capture the subtleties expressed in the indigenous languages; hence, some of the insight traditional knowledge may have to offer about indigenous plants, animals, and elements may be lost through translation (Johnson and Ruttan 1991).

In contrast to Western science, TEK is more holistic than reductionist, subjective rather than objective, and experiential rather than positivist (Wolfe et al. 1992). Because it is an oral-based knowledge system, it is often difficult to transmit ideas and concepts to those who do not share the tradition and the experience. For example, aboriginal hunters develop their concepts through their own experience as well as shared and familiar experiences with other members of the community. Any instruction they receive would be oral instruction from another person and rarely from pictures or the written word. Consequently, hunters find it difficult to describe their observations and ideas to someone versed in scientific explanation and unfamiliar with the traditional, cognitive system.

Often, TEK is revealed through stories and legends, making it difficult for nonaboriginal people to understand. Even the younger members of an aboriginal community may not know the proper way to approach an elder to discuss certain subjects. Likewise, they may be unfamiliar with all of the subtleties and sophisticated terms of the aboriginal language. Consequently, when speaking with an elder, a younger person may not know how to ask the proper questions to obtain specialized knowledge of the ecology, medicines, and spiritual matters (Colorado 1988; Johnson and Ruttan 1991).

Like Western science, TEK has its limitations. Unfortunately, some researchers tend to be overly romantic and uncritical of TEK. For example, although claims that spiritual explanations conceal conservation measures may be true in most cases, there are undoubtedly examples where a taboo on the hunting of a species may have a detrimental effect, perhaps by putting increased pressure on some other, more easily depleted species. Methods to improve fishing or hunting that focus on appeasing the spirits or counteracting the effects of sorcery may divert attention from the real and often correctable causes of the problem (Johannes 1992).

Aboriginal peoples are often reluctant to accept Western science because of what appears to be its fundamental need to control and interfere with nature. Scientists are viewed to be constantly tagging and capturing animals or digging holes in the ground. There is no denying the socially and ecologically destructive impact of Western science and technology on aboriginal cultures. However, in some instances, the technology of Western science may be able to provide information that is otherwise unavailable through TEK — for example, the ability to view phenomena at the microscopic level or over large distances.

To remedy this situation, local people must become directly involved in the research. In doing so, they will better understand the reasons for the experiments. This leads to the third problem of integration, the need to break down cultural barriers through collaboration between aboriginal and nonaboriginal researchers.

## Cultural and Disciplinary Barriers

Traditional environmental knowledge must be documented by aboriginal peoples themselves. This "inside" perspective is essential if the information is to be interpreted accurately. Moreover, it is a fundamental right of aboriginal peoples, or any local people for that matter, to have control over research that directly affects them. At the same time, if the goal is to integrate TEK and Western science, both social and natural scientists must assist in interpreting results from a Western scientific perspective.

Perceptual and language barriers between aboriginal and non-aboriginal researchers are often significant. To overcome these obstacles, training for both aboriginal and nonaboriginal researchers is necessary. All too often, it is the aboriginal researcher who is taught the scientific method and forced to adapt his or her cultural reality to that model. Western scientists need the same exposure to the knowledge system of the aboriginal group they are working with. Only when both groups develop an appreciation of, and sensitivity to, the strengths and limitations of their respective knowledge systems can integration begin to occur.

In addition to the cultural barriers between aboriginal and non-aboriginal researchers, methodological barriers exist between social and natural scientists. The traditional anthropological methods of interviewing and participant observation are often perceived by natural scientists as lacking scientific rigour in their analyses. Even though it is essential that TEK research involve people with appropriate backgrounds in biology, ecology, and resource management, it is also essential to include people with social science skills. Traditional environmental knowledge cannot be properly understood if it is analyzed independently of the social and political structure in which it is imbedded. The social perspective includes the way people perceive, use, allocate, transfer, and manage their natural resources (Johannes 1992). Traditional environmental knowledge is based on an oral tradition and concerned primarily with qualitative observations. Gathering both biological data and information about the local sociopolitical structure can best be accomplished through talking with people and participating directly in harvesting activities. Social scientists bring these skills to TEK research along with their ability to help translate information from one culture to another.

## Political Power

The final problem of integration is to develop institutional arrangements that recognize the validity of both TEK and Western science and are just in their distribution of authority. Currently, comanagement regimes represent the most widespread attempt to integrate TEK and Western science. Osherenko (1988, p. 13) defined comanagement as follows:

> A co-management regime is an institutional arrangement in which government agencies with jurisdiction over resources and user groups enter into an agreement covering a specific geographic region and spelling out: 1) a system of rights and obligations for those interested in the resource; 2) a collection of rules indicating actions that subjects are expected to take under various circumstances; and 3) procedures for making collective decisions affecting the interests of government actors, user organizations, and individual users.

For aboriginal peoples, comanagement represents an incremental step toward local self-government. There are now seven wildlife comanagement regimes in the North American arctic; several others are in various stages of conception (Osherenko 1988). These include the James Bay and northern Quebec hunting, fishing, and trapping regime; the Alaskan whaling regime (Bering and Beaufort seas; Alaskan whaling communities); the Beverly and Kaminuriak caribou management regime (central Canadian Arctic); the Inuvialuit wildlife harvesting and management regime (Inuvialuit Settlement Region within the Northwest Territories); the beluga management regime (northern Quebec); the Canadian porcupine caribou herd management regime (northwestern Canada, Yukon Territory, and Northwest Territories); and the Pacific walrus regime (coastal areas of northwestern Alaska). These regimes vary in their structure and in the degree of power accorded the participating groups.

Most of these comanagement regimes have existed for less than a decade; hence, it is difficult to draw any firm conclusions regarding their degree of success or failure. From her evaluation of the Beverly–Kaminuriak Caribou Management Plan, the Northern Quebec Beluga Management Plan, and the Yukon–Kuskokwim Delta Goose Management Plan in Alaska, Osherenko (1988) concludes that comanagement has at least improved the communication and understanding between aboriginal and nonaboriginal authorities. In addition, the cases suggest that comanagement has changed hunting practices in the interests of protecting declining species.

Nevertheless, despite the obvious step forward in bringing Western science and TEK together to help solve environmental problems, these boards have only an advisory capacity. The question remains to what extent they actually incorporate new innovative strategies to problem solving, as opposed to using TEK merely to provide data for a decentralized state system, which continues to adhere to the scientific paradigm and to do the managing. Will these boards serve as a model for comprehensive wildlife management under land claims settlements? If they do, there are many problems they will have to resolve. What will be the framework for making decisions, including the measures that will be used to evaluate any data collected? Who will have the ultimate authority, the state or the local resource users?

## Conclusions

It is clear that the integration of the two knowledge systems — TEK and Western science — remains a distant goal. However, if it is to occur, the following conditions must be met:

- *Support for the comprehensive documentation of TEK:* Sufficient financial and adequate administrative support at the political, bureaucratic, scientific, and local levels must be made available to support the documentation of TEK before it is lost.

- *Recognition of alternative knowledge systems:* Governments and the scientific community must work to develop an environmental assessment and management process that is flexible enough to accommodate new ideas and methods and that accepts Western science as only one method of seeking new knowledge and new interpretations of that knowledge. New and innovative resource-management programs must be given the necessary financial and administrative support to allow them to flourish.

🐾 *Support for cross-cultural education of both Western scientists and aboriginal peoples:* Training programs and hands-on learning must be available to both groups to introduce them to each other's knowledge system.

🐾 *Political recognition of aboriginal claims to land and resources:* Aboriginal peoples must be fully involved in the design and production of any future resource-management schemes; they must be recognized through their participation with equal authority and legal standing.

## References

Berkes, F. 1977. Fishery resource use in a sub-Arctic Indian community. Human Ecology, 5(4), 289–309.

_____1988. Environmental philosophy of the Chisasibi Cree People of James Bay. *In* Freeman, M.M.R., Carbyn, L.N., ed., Traditional knowledge and renewable resource management. Boreal Institute for Northern Studies, Edmonton, Alta., Canada. Occasional Publication No. 23, pp. 7–21.

_____1992. Traditional ecological knowledge in perspective. Natural Resources Institute, Winnipeg, Man., Canada.

Berlin, B. 1973. Folk systematics in relation to biological classification and nomenclature. Annual Review of Ecology and Systematics, 4, 259–271.

Booth, A., Jacobs, H.M. 1990. Ties that bind: native American beliefs as a foundation for environmental consciousness. Environmental Ethics, 12, 27–43.

Brody, H. 1981. Maps and dreams: Indians and the British Columbia frontier. Douglas and McIntyre, Toronto, Ont., Canada.

Bulmer, R. 1970. Which came first, the chicken or the egghead? *In* Pouillon, J., Maranda, P., ed., Echanges et communications. Vol. II. Mouton and Co., The Hague, Netherlands. pp. 1069–1091.

Capra, F. 1982. The turning point: science, society and the rising culture. Bantam Books, Toronto, Ont., Canada.

Colorado, P. 1988. Bridging Western and native science. Convergence, 21(2/3).

Diamond, J.M. 1966. Zoological classification system of a primitive people. Science, 151, 1102–1104.

Feit, H. 1973. The ethno-ecology of the Waswanipi Cree: or how hunters can manage their resources. In Cox, B., ed., Cultural ecology. McClelland and Stewart, Toronto, Ont., Canada. pp. 115–125.

_____1986. James Bay Cree Indian management and moral considerations of fur bearers. In Native people and renewable resource management. Alberta Society of Professional Biologists, Edmonton, Alta., Canada. pp. 49–65.

_____1988. Self-management and state-management: forms of knowing and managing northern wildlife. In Freeman, M.M.R., Carbyn, L.N., ed., Traditional knowledge and renewable resource management. Boreal Institute for Northern Studies, Edmonton, Alta., Canada. Occasional Publication No. 23, pp. 72–91.

Gunn, A., Arlooktoo, G., Kaomayak, D. 1988. The contribution of ecological knowledge of Inuit to wildlife management in the Northwest Territories. In Freeman, M.M.R., Carbyn, L.N., ed., Traditional knowledge and renewable resource management. Boreal Institute for Northern Studies, Edmonton, Alta., Canada. Occasional Publication No. 23, pp. 22–29.

Hunn, E. 1975. Cognitive processes in folk-ornithology: the identification of gulls. Language-Behaviour Research Laboratory, University of California, Berkeley, CA, USA. Working Paper No. 42, 73 pp.

Irving, L. 1960. Birds of Anaktuvuk Pass, Kobuk and Old Crow. United States National Museum, Washington, DC, USA. Bulletin 217.

IUCN (International Union for the Conservation of Nature and Natural Resources). 1986. Tradition, conservation and development. IUCN, Morges, Switzerland. Occasional Newsletter of the Commission on Ecology's Working Group on Traditional Ecological Knowledge, No. 4.

IUCN (International Union for the Conservation of Nature and Natural Resources), UNEP (United Nations Environment Programme), and WWF (World Wildlife Fund). 1980. World conservation strategy. IUCN, Morges, Switzerland.

Johnson, M. 1987. Inuit folk-ornithology in the Povungnituk Region of northern Quebec. Department of Anthropology, University of Toronto, Toronto, Ont., Canada. MA thesis.

Johnson, M., Ruttan, R. 1991. Dene traditional environmental knowledge: pilot project. Dene Cultural Institute, Hay River, NWT, Canada.

Johannes, R.E. 1992. Integrating traditional ecological knowledge and management with environmental assessment. Natural Resources Institute, Winnipeg, Man., Canada. In press.

Johannes, R.E., Ruddle, K., Hviding, E. 1991. The value today of traditional management and knowledge of coastal marine resources in Oceania. *In* Proceedings of the 2nd Regional Technical Meeting on Fisheries, Nouméa, New Caledonia, 5–9 August 1991. South Pacific Commission, Nouméa, New Caledonia.

Jones, N.B., Konner, M.J. 1989. !Kung knowledge of animal behaviour. *In* Johannes, R., ed., Traditional ecological knowledge: a collection of essays. International Union for the Conservation of Nature and Natural Resources, Morges, Switzerland.

Mulvihill, P. 1988. Integration of the state and indigenous systems of wildlife management: problems and possibilities. School of Urban and Regional Planning, Faculty of Environmental Studies, University of Waterloo, Waterloo, Ont., Canada.

Nakashima, D. 1990. Application of native knowledge in EIA: Inuit eiders and Hudson Bay oil. Canadian Environmental Assessment Research Council, Hull, Que., Canada.

Nelson, R. 1983. Make prayers to the raven: a Koyukon view of the northern forest. University of Chicago Press, Chicago, IL, USA.

Osherenko, G. 1988. Sharing power with native users: co-management regimes for Arctic wildlife. Canadian Arctic Resources Committee, Ottawa, Ont., Canada. CARC Policy Paper 5.

Snyder, L.L. 1957. Arctic birds of Canada. University of Toronto Press, Toronto, Ont., Canada.

Usher, P.J. 1986. Devolution of power in the Northwest Territories: *In* Native people and renewable resource management. Proceedings of the Alberta Society of Professional Biologists. Alberta Society of Professional Biologists, Edmonton, Alta., Canada. pp. 69–80.

WCED (World Commission on Environment and Development). 1987. Our common future. Oxford University Press, Oxford, UK. 400 pp.

Wolfe, J., Bechard, C., Cizek, P., Cole, D. 1992. Indigenous and Western knowledge and resource management systems. University of Guelph, Guelph, Ont., Canada. Rural Reportings, Native Canadian Issues Series, 1.

# The Workshop:
# Purpose and Results

The idea to hold an international workshop on the documentation and application of traditional environmental knowledge
(TEK) arose through the joint interest of the International Development Research Centre (IDRC) and the Dene Cultural Institute
(DCI). In July 1990, nongovernmental groups from Canada's
North, the South Pacific, the African Sahel, northern Thailand,
and elsewhere came together to share their experiences. Most of
these groups use a participatory action approach to research and
involve both aboriginal and nonaboriginal researchers.

In the year leading up to the workshop, DCI conducted a pilot
project to document TEK in the Dene community of Fort Good
Hope in Canada's Northwest Territories. Originally, the workshop was to be held in Fort Good Hope; however, given the
theme, local community researchers suggested that it be held in
a traditional Dene camp. Pursuing this idea, DCI and the community of Fort Good Hope began to establish a camp along the
shores of the Mackenzie River. Their guests, from the far corners
of the globe, would sleep in tents on beds of spruce bows, sample
fresh fish and caribou, and experience the breathtaking scenery
of this majestic river.

By Martha Johnson, Dene Cultural Institute, Yellowknife, NWT, Canada.

*Workshop participants at the Mackenzie River camp.*

The biggest challenge of the workshop was to stimulate open discussion and interaction to draw out the common and distinct aspects of each project. With such a disparate group, each participant with different motivations, agendas, and cultural backgrounds, this was not an easy task. In addition to the project representatives, participants included local Dene elders, interested community members, various independent social and natural scientists, and government employees.

The workshop was the first of its kind to bring together aboriginal and nonaboriginal researchers from around the world in a unique cultural setting. For those participants not used to the cold weather, rustic facilities, and long hours of daylight, it meant some discomfort. Visits from local community residents, boat rides down the river, and all-night drum dances introduced the guests to Dene culture and provided an ideal forum for people to share their experiences in an informal setting. However, people who tried to sleep to be up early for the workshop missed out on the cultural experience and those who stayed up most of the night were too tired to work the next day. Inclement weather, leaky tents, lack of sleep and the many activities going on in camp often distracted from the job at hand. Nevertheless, an agenda did evolve and the work got done.

## *The Presentations: A Summary*

The workshop was organized around the case studies presented by each group. In most instances, presentations were jointly made by collaborating aboriginal and nonaboriginal researchers. In the case of the Dene project, elders who had participated as advisors on the project also spoke, giving those present a real taste of the traditional Dene view of the world.

Most presenters concentrated on the research process of their respective projects and outlined efforts to apply the information gathered. However, a few focused on the impact of Western acculturation on their traditional knowledge and their political struggle to achieve self-determination. This disturbed some of the participants, who saw the workshop, with its focus on research methodology and application, as an inappropriate forum for political speeches. On the other hand, the recognition of aboriginal land rights and self-government are fundamental issues in the struggle to preserve and apply traditional knowledge and cannot be ignored in the broader sociopolitical context. The social dynamics of the workshop in effect reflected the whole cultural and political reality of traditional environmental knowledge research as well as the underlying power struggles and opposing world views that are a part of it.

### *The DCI Pilot Project*

The DCI report describes and evaluates a pilot project to document traditional environmental knowledge. Initiated by an aboriginal organization, the goal of the project is to collect as much traditional information as quickly as possible before it is lost with the disappearance of the current generation of elders. Eventually, the information will be used for education and environmental management, but precise applications have yet to be determined. The methodology emphasizes the use of a semi-structured questionnaire in the Dene language to gather information about the behaviour of different animal species and traditional rules of management. Local researchers receive training in basic research skills, are involved in designing the questionnaires, and carry out the interviews. The evaluation of the pilot project stresses the need for more direct community control of research, a greater role for elders in interpreting results, and the need for more cooperation and sharing of knowledge between scientists and local researchers.

## The Belcher Islands Project

The Belcher Islands project is a collaborative, community-based research initiative involving the Inuit community of Sanikiluaq and scientists from the Canadian Circumpolar Institute. The traditional environmental knowledge of the Inuit is combined with Western science to develop a cooperative management plan for a herd of reindeer recently introduced to the Belcher Islands. A variety of methods are used to document TEK, including participation in hunting activities, community meetings, informal discussions, and formal interviews.

## The Marovo Lagoon Project

The Marovo Lagoon project is an initiative of the Marovo community, with some government guidance and support. Although the project did not arise specifically to document TEK, this is a vitally important element of the research. A key feature of the Marovo project is its focus on information exchange rather than formal interviewing. The research is reciprocal in nature. Visiting investigators are invited to apply their skills and knowledge in ways relevant to the project. They are encouraged to learn traditional skills and information through hands-on experience and to promote feedback of TEK in documented form to stimulate the interest of informants and make others more aware of its nature and extent. The on-site research process is characterized by a loosely formulated structure of "informal" research administration: elders, local project staff, interviewers, interpreters, and other villagers guide visiting investigators to the topics and locations deemed to be important from a local perspective.

## The Sahel Oral History Project

The Sahel project also has an applied focus. The report describes how traditional knowledge about ecological change and past agricultural and conservation techniques can directly benefit a development project: in this case, the implementation of a community forestry program. Like the Dene research, the aim of this project is not only to record indigenous knowledge and determine how to involve the elderly and other local people directly in the research process but also to develop a practical methodology that could be incorporated into project planning, implementation, and evaluation. With the information collected, some direct applications are planned. They include developing an index to provide easy access to comments made on topical political, social, and economic issues; development education; botanical and agricultural surveys; and guidelines for extension workers.

## The Highlanders of Northern Thailand

From northern Thailand, and the Mountain People's Culture and Development Educational Programme (MPCDE), there are two reports. The first discusses an IDRC-sponsored project examining the impact of regional development on the highlanders of northern Thailand. Here, as with the Marovo Lagoon and Sahel projects, TEK research is only one component of a larger study. Traditional environmental knowledge is examined in light of how it has adapted to ecological and social changes and to what extent it has been incorporated into development ventures. Data is collected by local researchers through informal interviews. The information is then compiled into tables designed by the administrative research team for comparative analysis.

The second paper describes efforts made by MPCDE, since its inception in 1980, to document and apply traditional environmental knowledge among the highlanders of northern Thailand. Research to date has focused on the Akha people. Unlike the other projects, the MPCDE project does not always make a clear distinction between ecological, managerial, historical, or ritual knowledge; they are regarded as being interwoven into all aspects of cultural life. The most important feature of the MPCDE research is that it is not intended for "outside" publication. Rather, it is meant to create awareness of existing development problems and their possible solutions among participating team members, interviewers, informants, and villagers.

## Other Presentations

Two other presentations were made: one by an individual from the Amazon Basin and another on the comanagement agreements in Washington State, USA. As these presentations were of a less formal nature, no reports are included in this book. Synopses of the presentations appear in the Appendix.

## The Discussions

Following the presentations, participants formed small groups and attempted to draw out the common threads of each project with respect to research methodology and application. Despite initial suggestions to form small working groups focusing on specific topics early on in the workshop, in retrospect, it was necessary to hear the case studies first. Not everyone was able to read the draft papers before the workshop. Further, discussions following the presentations allowed for a lively interchange of information between participants. Later, when participants did break up into small groups they had a clear understanding of all the projects, which allowed for better comparison.

Despite the range of project orientations and vastly different sociopolitical and ecological situations, many common elements emerged from the workshop. Dr Evelyn Pinkerton acted as the workshop rapporteur. In the final section of this book, she summarizes the discussions surrounding each of the presentations and identifies some of the issues that participants viewed as essential, common elements of TEK research. These include the land tenure situation, the major problem or dilemma traditional environmental knowledge is expected to correct, methods, and traditional environmental knowledge as both a long-term and a short-term strategy. Many other important issues emerged from the presentations and discussions. These include the problem of defining traditional environmental knowledge, the problem of translating one world view into another, the role of outside collaborators in TEK research, the need for increased dialogue between social and natural scientists, and the problems of applying traditional knowledge in a modern context.

## *Observations and Conclusions*

An important outcome of the workshop was the realization that, because of the different orientations and goals of the projects, they were difficult to compare. For instance, the Dene and Thai projects were initiated by aboriginal peoples to document TEK as quickly as possible before it is lost — once the information is collected, ways would be found to apply it to education and resource management. Others, like the Marovo Lagoon and Belcher Islands projects, emphasize collaboration between scientists and local people to study specific research problems. The African Sahel project was different again: it was actually a sideline to a larger development project initiated by an outside agency.

The sociopolitical and ecological contexts of each project also had a profound impact on their outcomes and, hence, the extent to which the application of TEK could be compared among the different groups. It appears that the degree of autonomy held by an aboriginal group and the impact of assimilation on that group ultimately affects the status of their traditional knowledge. For instance, in the Solomon Islands, the indigenous people own most of the land and the majority still speak the aboriginal languages. This situation is very different from that of the Dene, who, at the time of the workshop, still held no legally recognized title to their land and face an uphill battle to preserve the rapid erosion of their languages and culture.

The type of traditional knowledge being collected also differed between groups. The Thai group took a much broader, holistic interpretation of traditional knowledge than did the Dene or the Marovo Lagoon researchers. Ecological knowledge was an important focus of the Thai study; however, it was gathered along with information about other aspects of hill tribe cultures, such as traditional medicine, justice, and religion. The Belcher Islands project was also unique as it involved reindeer introduced to a region that had been without caribou or reindeer for about a century.

The workshop explored a full range of issues related to traditional environmental knowledge and helped participants to situate their work within this range. However, participants learned that they were in very different situations and that what they could compare at this point was limited. Because of the vastly different contexts, most participants felt it was difficult to generalize about the research and premature to make recommendations about management systems. In some sense, this amounted to a recognition that it is perhaps more appropriate to take on one issue at a time: data management, indexing systems, etc.

Tasks suggested as part of future networking included exchanging questionnaires, reviewing the types of collaboration that seem successful, more clearly identifying what type of TEK research is being done, and continuing to educate the public and resource-management agencies about traditional environmental knowledge. In countries such as Brazil, where traditional environmental knowledge is not recognized, international conferences and film crews should be used to document the use of traditional resources. In all countries, the marketing of value-added products that represent a more complete use of subsistence goods (for example, caribou hides) should be developed. Finally, to make the public more aware of TEK, it must be linked to the issue of sustainable resource management. Sustainability is part of the very definition of traditional environmental knowledge.

# CANADA'S NORTH

*The following two case studies from the Dene Cultural Institute and the Belcher Island Adaptive Reindeer Management Project describe two very different experiences from Canada's North. The first paper, by Martha Johnson and Robert Ruttan of DCI, describes and evaluates a pilot project to document traditional environmental knowledge. The goal of the project is to collect as much tradtional wisdom as quickly as possible, before it is lost with the passing of the Dene elders. The second paper, by Miriam McDonald Fleming, provides a status report on a comanagement plan, integrating traditional Inuit wisdom and Western science, for a herd of reindeer recently introduced to Canada's Belcher Islands.*

# Traditional Environmental Knowledge of the Dene: A Pilot Project

The Dene occupy a vast geographical area in the Northwest Territories covering 1 million square kilometres and spanning several different geographical regions (The Dene Nation 1984). The name they give to their land is *Denendeh*, or "Land of the People." For administrative purposes, Denendeh is divided into five regions: the Gwich'in Settlement Area, Sahtu, Deh Cho, North Slave, and South Slave (Fig. 1). The cultural groups represented are distinguished according to their linguistic affiliation, and include the Gwich'in, the North and South Slavey, the Dogrib, and the Chipewyan. Currently, only the Gwich'in have reached a land-claim settlement with the Canadian Federal Government. Negotiations with the other groups continue.

Central to the existence of the Dene has been their relationship with the land. For thousands of years, this land of mountains, lakes, rivers, tundra, and forests dominated by a subarctic climate, has supported the Dene people through hunting, trapping, and fishing. Centuries of experience in living off the land have

By Martha Johnson and Robert A. Ruttan, Dene Cultural Institute, Yellowknife, NWT, Canada.

endowed the Dene with an intimate knowledge of the geography and resources that have sustained them for generations and remain central to Dene life today.

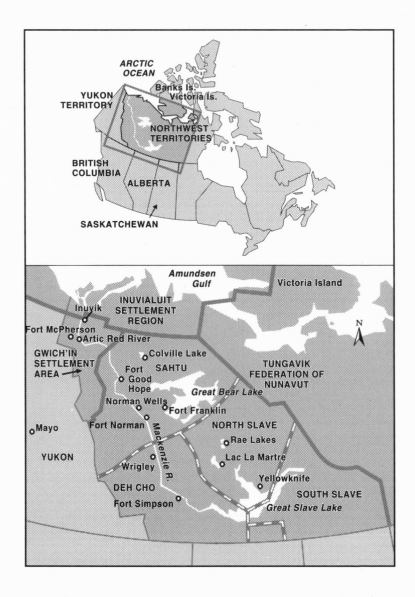

*Fig. 1. The western Northwest Territories of Canada, the land of the Dene.*

In 1987, 200 delegates representing the 26 communities and the 14 thousand people of Denendeh met to discuss their concerns about the future of their culture. The outcome of the conference was the formation of the Dene Cultural Institute. Its mandate is to preserve and promote Dene culture through the coordination of research and educational activities. Traditional environmental knowledge (TEK) was chosen as the first area for major research because of the central role the land plays in Dene culture and because this knowledge is fast disappearing with the passing of Dene elders.

The documentation of Dene traditional environmental knowledge is a formidable undertaking given the extent of that knowledge, the vast area that must be covered, and the different languages and cultures involved. In addition to these obstacles, there have been few precedents set to document traditional knowledge using a participatory community approach to research. With so little experience to draw upon, the Dene Cultural Institute decided to begin its research with a 1-year pilot project to take place in a representative community before expanding the research into other Denendeh communities. Fort Good Hope (Radeli Ko), located along the Mackenzie River in the North Slavey region, was chosen for the pilot project. The neighbouring community of Colville Lake (K'ahabamitue), which has strong kinship ties to Fort Good Hope, was also included in the study.

The pilot project began in August 1989 and continued intermittently through 1991. Its purpose was twofold: first, to develop a participatory action research methodology to document TEK and, second, to gain an understanding of environmental knowledge still possessed by Dene and how this knowledge has been used to govern their use of the land and its resources. This paper describes and evaluates the methodology that was developed and tested and provides a brief overview of the results.

# Research on Traditional Environmental Knowledge

The primary objective of TEK research is to document the knowledge of surviving elders for both cultural preservation and use by younger Dene. In addition, one of the long-term goals of the Dene Cultural Institute is to integrate TEK with Western science to aid in future resource management. The first step in achieving this goal is to understand the nature and scope of Dene traditional environmental knowledge and the system of management that governed the Dene's use of resources in the past and that continues to evolve today. The Institute identified several key questions for the documentation of TEK. They included the following:

- What kinds of traditional environmental knowledge do people still possess and how was this knowledge used to survive and to live in harmony with the natural environment?

- What are the practices and beliefs that are essential to Dene resource management, and how are they similar or different from those of Euro-Canadian society or other indigenous cultures?

- To what extent is a "traditional" Dene system of resource management still in existence today?

- Is there more than one system currently operating today, and, if so, what are the social, cultural, economic, and environmental factors that define them?

The Dene Cultural Institute hoped that the pilot project would shed some light on these questions; however, its major purpose was to develop a participatory action research methodology to document Dene traditional environmental knowledge. Accordingly, the following objectives were outlined:

- Develop methods of data collection to determine the scope and nature of TEK in a typical Dene community; to ascertain

the available ecological information concerning certain
important species; and to develop an understanding of the
systems of traditional management that govern their use by
Dene.

ها Develop and test a training program to provide local researchers with basic research skills in social science and ecology.

ها Create a system of data management for information on
traditional knowledge.

ها Determine how to involve local government, elders, and other
knowledgeable community members in developing and
administrating participatory action research.

ها Develop appropriate methods to disseminate traditional
knowledge to Dene communities, scholarly and professional
communities, and the general public.

ها Establish a cooperative working relationship with other institutions conducting similar research.


## *Project Development*

### *Obtaining community support*

Following the local channels of authority, the Executive Director
of the Dene Cultural Institute met with the Band Council of Fort
Good Hope to discuss the goals of the research and to obtain the
Council's support for the pilot project. Upon giving their consent,
the Band Council agreed to help select the local researchers and
members of the Steering Committee. Aside from these tasks and
helping the Research Director and Project Biologist to secure
accommodation, the Band Council had no direct involvement
with the adminstration of the project.

Although the Band Council approved and supported the program
and the community researchers and informants publicized the

project at every opportunity, the community at large expressed little interest in the research. Even though this problem might be solved by more community meetings before and during the research, the research team recommended that a Community Administrative Committee be appointed to develop community interest and provide continuity and direction to future research. The Committee would be composed of representatives from the community identified by the Band Council and a representative of the Dene Cultural Institute. The latter would play only an advisory role to the Committee and would liaise between the community and the Institute. The Committee would have the following responsibilities:

* Define the duties and responsibilities of the community and the role of the Dene Cultural Institute with respect to the administration of funds, payment schedules, control of information, reporting, and evaluation of project.

* Publicize the project within the community and elsewhere.

* Outline the work process, including the work plan, research methodology, and training needs.

* Select community and outside researchers, Elders' Council (Steering Committee), and Technical Advisory Committee and define their respective duties or responsibilities.

* Arrange for office space and training facilities for the project and housing for outside researchers if necessary.

* Monitor the progress of the project through regular meetings with the community, outside researchers, and the Elders' Council.

## Steering Committee

The Steering Committee was made up of six elders. Members were chosen jointly by the Band Council and the community researchers. The Committee was to guide the research team in the subjects to be investigated, to aid in interpreting the findings, and to publicize the project within the community. Two Steering Committee meetings were held during the initial planning stage to discuss research subjects. Two further meetings were held during the following year to update members on work progress and to obtain feedback from them about the research. Meetings were conducted in North Slavey and English, with the community researchers acting as interpreters for the outside researchers.

In retrospect, the research team felt that the Steering Committee did not fulfil its intended role and was not used effectively. Although these elders were keenly interested in the project, they did not provide the expected direction in the choice of research subjects or culturally appropriate methods of obtaining required information. Thus, the first meetings consisted mainly of descriptions of the "proposed" project with suggestions for research subjects being made by the research team and approved by the Steering Committee. In subsequent meetings, the Committee members, now more familiar with the project, more actively voiced their opinions and concerns, which assisted researchers in revising questionnaires and improving interview techniques. However, final decisions concerning research methods were made almost entirely by the Research Director and the Project Biologist in consultation with community researchers and the Executive Director of the Dene Cultural Institute.

Experience led the research team to believe that the Steering Committee should have been more actively and regularly involved in the training program and the interpretation of data. The research team thus recommended that an Elders' Advisory Council be established. As most traditional environmental knowledge is held by the older community members, this advisory body could provide valuable assistance in interpreting language and data as well as suggesting important areas of research. An Elders' Council would also help to restore the traditional role of elders as community teachers and advisors, respected for their knowledge and wisdom.

## Community researchers

Three community researchers were selected by the Band Council
in consultation with the Dene Cultural Institute. They were
chosen primarily on the basis of their fluency in English and
North Slavey, knowledge of their culture, previous research experience, and their interest and motivation.

At the outset, all the researchers were female; but when one of
the women was unable to continue, she was replaced by a man
who remained for the duration of the project. Although gender
was not a factor in selecting local researchers, it was recognized
that, to have all views represented, both men and women should
be on the research team. One of the most experienced female
researchers pointed out that, as a younger woman gathering
information in a traditionally male domain, it took some time to
establish her credibility and gain the confidence of some of the
male elders.

The research team concluded that lack of experience and linguistic skills could be overcome through more intensive training in
both research and language, combined with a cooperative working relationship or team approach. A qualified interpreter as a
team member would also be an asset.

Other problems encountered during the pilot project were attri-
tion or absenteeism resulting from lack of commitment, pressing
family responsibilities, and personal problems (such as alcohol
abuse). The research team felt that these problems would be
resolved through careful selection, direction, and supervision of
the community researchers by the Community Administrative
Committee.

One of the biggest problems encountered in both training and
research was the community researchers' lack of fluency in both
English and North Slavey, compounded by the outside
researchers' ignorance of North Slavey. Unless community
researchers were fluent in both English and North Slavey, they
could not participate effectively in all phases of the research. It

was recognized that local researchers must achieve oral proficiency and written literacy in their own language to communicate better with their informants and to be able to transcribe the information accurately. At the same time, local researchers must be proficient enough in English to be able to do effective translation. In future, they may also be required to write funding proposals and reports as well as make public presentations.

Previous experience was viewed as a desirable quality for community researchers. However, in practice, it was found that experienced researchers did not necessarily perform better than inexperienced people when the latter possessed a high level of enthusiasm for the work.

During and after brief periods of instruction in basic ecology and social science research methods, the local and outside researchers worked cooperatively to design and test questionnaires for ethnographic interviews. The researchers then conducted, translated, and transcribed the subsequent interviews and participated in interpreting the results. They also assisted in evaluating the project, developing recommendations for improved methodology, and promoting the project within the community.

## Outside professional researchers

From the point of view of Western science, TEK is a multidisciplinary field of study involving ecology, geography, anthropology, and linguistics. Given the goal of the Dene Cultural Institute to further the integration of traditional knowledge and Western science, a social scientist (the Research Director of the Dene Cultural Institute) and an experienced biologist were hired to provide a Western scientific perspective to the research and to deliver the training program.

Over an 18-month period beginning in August 1989, the outside researchers made six trips to the community, spending a total of 4 months training and working with the local researchers. This was not enough time to provide both adequate training of local researchers and required on-the-spot analysis of collected information. On average, it required at least 1 week of each trip to deal with administrative and personnel problems, and to review the work the local researchers had been doing, before any further training or data collection could begin. In the absence of a full-time experienced researcher, problems that arose could not be promptly resolved.

Time constraints also prevented the outside researchers from taking part in, or observing, traditional activities (such as fishing, trapping, and the spring hunt), which would have provided insight into traditional knowledge in the appropriate social context and a greater understanding of its value and application. Lack of hands-on experience may lead the outside researcher to make incorrect assumptions about the quality of information or the way it is used. Such assumptions and cultural biases have always been detrimental to both understanding and effective cooperation between native and "foreign" agencies and individuals. Having both outside and community researchers work as a team can help both groups recognize potential cultural biases and common misunderstandings and so resolve them through collaborative discussion.

Besides providing a Western scientific perspective to the research, the outside researcher also acted as an "outside observer." There were times during the pilot project when community researchers saw little value in asking certain questions because "the answer was too obvious." The answer was such and integral part of their cultural understanding that it seemed to them to be common knowledge. Yet, for the outsider, or the "uninitiated" younger Dene, the answers to these questions are often the key to understanding traditional knowledge.

In future work involving experienced community researchers, the role of outside researchers could be reduced. They could be limited to assisting in the analysis of TEK and in its integration with Western science as a basis of sustainable resource management.

## Technical Advisory Committee

A Technical Advisory Committee was established by the Dene Cultural Institute to ensure a critical review of the research from a professional standpoint as well as to provide new ideas and insights into the work. The Committee was composed of academics and other professionals with experience in the biological and social sciences and in participatory action research. Its members helped develop the original project proposal by providing advice on research questions and suggesting methods for data collection, and are expected to participate in evaluating the pilot project's final report. Also, questionnaires and transcripts were circulated among Committee members for comments. In retrospect, the value of the Technical Advisory Committee would have been enhanced by more frequent contact with all members of the research team.

## Selection of informants

A preliminary list of potential informants was put together by the Steering Committee in consultation with the community researchers. Informants from Fort Good Hope and Colville Lake were selected according to their experience in living off the land and their recognized knowledge of traditional life. Most were elders, but a few younger, middle-aged people were also interviewed.

The research team believed that the older generation was the better source of traditional knowledge; however, they agreed that anyone who had spent a significant portion of their life "on the land" accompanied by parents or as independent hunters, trappers, or fishers would have accumulated much valuable knowledge of the natural environment. It was important that both women and men be interviewed. Dene women may not have participated to the same extent as men in all traditional activities, but they are still knowledgeable about life on the land. They have heard the same stories and legends, which transmit traditional environmental knowledge, and have listened to discussions of male elders throughout their lives. Also, they may have specialized traditional knowledge that men do not possess (knowledge of medicinal plants, roots, berries, and small game, for example). As some individuals in a Dene community are recognized as being particularly knowledgeable or expert on certain geographical areas or particular species, it is important to interview a wide range of informants to ensure that different perspectives are represented.

## Community researcher training program

The objective of the training program was to provide community researchers with an ample understanding of social research methods and ecology. This knowledge would then allow them to ask appropriate questions from a scientific perspective and translate acquired information into meaningful English. The pilot project was expected to provide insight and guidelines that could serve as the basis for more sophisticated research training in the future.

Time and resources were inadequate to develop a formal training program in advance. It soon became apparent, however, that any effective training program required frequent adjustment to meet the individual needs of the community researchers, whose formal education, command of English, and personal experience with the subject matter varied widely and was generally limited. Thus, the training program was, to a degree, as much a learning process for the "instructors" as it was for the "students": the students' responses gave the instructors insight into the best methods of teaching these subjects to adults with limited academic education and no scientific training.

Most of the formal academic training occurred during the first month of the project, when outside researchers introduced the basic principles, concepts, and terminology of ecology, modern wildlife management, and social science research. About 2 weeks into the training, the research team began designing questionnaires for data collection. Short field trips were taken around the

community to observe some of the ecological topics to be studied; however, time constraints prevented extensive field observation. During subsequent visits to Fort Good Hope by outside
researchers, basic ecological concepts were reviewed, questions
arising from interviews were discussed, and questionnaires and
interview techniques were revised. From this exercise, subsequent interviews, translations, and transcriptions were
improved.

In evaluating the training program, the research team agreed that
1 month of classroom instruction was insufficient to provide
local researchers with adequate training. Instructors were able to
cover only the basic concepts and principles of ecology and social
science research. There was little time to introduce trainees to
forest and fisheries ecology, map reading, basic geomorphology,
land use planning, basic anatomy, and the use of computers, all
of which are important subjects for any kind of environmental
research. Further, the training program focused largely on Western science. Although elders were included on some of the short
field trips, they did not play a significant role in the training.
Hence, the Dene perspective was not formally integrated into the
learning process. The research team recommended that future
training programs include elders as well as scientists. It was also
recommended that future training programs emphasize field
training with elders as instructors.

# Documenting Dene Traditional Environmental Knowledge

## Developing methods of retrieval and documentation

For any group of people to sustain itself for countless generations
by harvesting wildlife, fish, and other resources or to manage
these resources in a modern context, it must have detailed
knowledge of the ecology of species to be harvested and the area
it occupies. Although documentation of ecological knowledge

should eventually encompass all species and other components of the Dene environment, this was not possible in the pilot project, which was designed to determine the type, quality, and scope of existing environmental knowledge and the principles and laws that governed traditional Dene use of resources in a sustainable manner. The problem was where and how to collect this information within the time frame of the pilot project.

The options were to examine the ecology of certain species and the principles for their sustainable harvest or to look at the ecological interrelationships of a particular ecosystem or "ecozone." After much discussion with the Steering Committee, it was decided that research should begin with the ecology of four important species: barren-ground caribou, moose, beaver, and marten. Caribou and moose have been major sources of food for countless generations of aboriginal people, and beaver and marten have been and are the most economically important fur-bearers of the region. Therefore, it was assumed that more knowledge would be associated with these important species than with less common species or those of lower cultural and economic value. After much discussion by the researchers, it was decided that information on taxonomy, basic biology, ecology, and management should be collected for each species.

Taxonomic information was sought, including species names, names of the different sexes, and age cohorts (fawn or kit, yearling, 2-year-old, and adult). This information was gathered not for a detailed taxonomic study, but rather to gain some insight into how the Dene perceive and use taxonomic relationships and associated nomenclature and how these compare with Western science. It was assumed that the use of correct North Slavey names for species would facilitate the interview process and ensure accurate identification of interspecific and other ecological relationships. Other information included habitat and habitat relationships, interspecific relationships, life cycles and reproduction, population dynamics, migrations and movements (of caribou and moose), parasites and diseases, and traditional and modern management (see *Beaver Questionnaire* at the end of this paper).

The research team decided that questions pertaining to traditional management should focus on traditional rules for hunting and trapping, including the special ways of showing respect for the animals. Based on their traditional knowledge, some informants were also asked about the best way to ensure the sustainable use of resources today, including the use of quotas for certain species, the designation of special seasons and areas for hunting and trapping, and the use and effects of modern technology, like snowmobiles and rifles.

## Methods of data collection

The primary method of data collection was the ethnographic interview, using a structured conversational approach. Together, the outside and community researchers formulated a series of open-ended questions. Local researchers were also encouraged to use participant observation when the opportunity arose, although no systematic study was done using this method.

A critical concern in developing questionnaires was to obtain data that would be important from both the Dene and scientific perspectives. Cultural bias was inevitable given that questions were formulated from a scientific perspective and then translated into North Slavey. However, local researchers were at least given the opportunity to exclude anything they felt to be unsuitable or to include questions of their own design. To identify any major problems, community researchers tested the first draft of one questionnaire before the outside researchers left the community.

Review of the first interview transcript revealed many superficial answers. Accordingly, questionnaires were revised: leading questions were removed, the sequence of topics was reorganized, and suggestions of the Technical Advisory Committee and regional and territorial biologists were incorporated. The review identified a need to avoid the use of abstract English words and concepts (such as "numerical," "trends," "evaluation," and "impact"), which were often difficult both to explain to the local researchers, with their limited understanding of English and Western science, and to translate into North Slavey. Community researchers also found that questions suggesting control of a species often elicited a negative reaction from informants because of the negative connotation that the idea of controlling wild species has in Dene culture. Similarly, informants were sometimes reluctant to divulge specific numbers of animals harvested. The community researchers explained that this was because some Dene considered discussion of hunting or trapping success to be bragging or feared the information might be used against them by the government.

Three months later, after a second set of interviews using the revised questionnaires, many of the responses were still superficial. Local researchers found that informants did not respond freely to a question–answer format. By constantly firing questions at an informant, they felt that they were restricting his or her freedom to address other issues that were of personal importance. Moreover, it was not clear to what extent the information gathered in this manner represented a Dene as opposed to Western perspective of the subjects being investigated.

After discussing these problems, the research team decided that a more open approach to questioning was needed. Henceforth, the questionnaire would serve merely as a checklist for the types of information being sought. Researchers were to allow the interview to flow as naturally as possible and not to worry about the order in which the information was elicited or whether all of the topics were covered during one interview. Interviewers began by asking a general opening question, something like "Can you tell me about beaver habitat in summer?" The idea was to give the informant the freedom to decide which subjects were important to talk about and to present the information in a way that he or she felt was most appropriate. Along with the opening question, the interviewer had a list of supplementary questions to ask should the informant be unresponsive or wander off topic.

Using specific local examples helped make the questioning more relevant to the experience of the informants. For instance, when inquiring about marten habitat, it helped to ask the informant to describe the physical characteristics of the trapping area.

The success of the "final" unstructured checklist method of interviewing depended primarily upon the skill of the interviewer to guide the conversation. Some informants required a lot of prodding to get them to talk. Others had a tendency to wander away from the subject or spend an inordinate amount of time discussing topics not directly related to the question. The more knowledgeable the interviewers were about the subject and the answers they were seeking from both a Dene and a scientific perspective, the better they were at extracting the desired kinds of information. This was more likely to occur if the interviewer reviewed the checklist thoroughly before the interview and thus maintained a relaxed dialogue with the informant without constantly having to look at the "checklist" or resort to a question–answer format.

One problem with gathering traditional knowledge from interviews in an artificial setting was that informants often had difficulty remembering and describing subject matter in accurate detail. For example, what species of willow are browsed by moose in the winter? Although the informant would know the North Slavey name for each of the preferred species, he or she could not describe them for the researcher without a specimen. During an instructional tour, one elder named several species of willow, shrub, and tree and described their values to the wildlife and the local people; however, in the absence of specimens, he could not distinguish between various species.

Another problem with the interview method was that it used Western scientific categories for the framework to collect information. This may not be the most effective method to elicit traditional knowledge. Much of the knowledge is transmitted in the form of stories and legends using metaphors and sophisticated Dene terminology that may not be well understood by younger interviewers. One community researcher frequently commented on the elders' use of "hidden words": North Slavey terms or metaphors, which were indirect references to certain animals or their behaviour, that could not be translated literally into English. Unless the interviewer is familiar with the stories and understands how to extract the ecological data from the narrative, an important source of information may be overlooked.

## Conducting the interview

### Preliminary interview

Before a formal interview, researchers made a brief introductory visit to each informant to explain the objectives of the project, what would happen to the information recorded, and the types of questions that would be asked during the actual interview. Informants were also given the opportunity to identify which animals they felt most knowledgeable to discuss. Once these preliminaries had been settled, a time and a place for the interview was established.

### Setting and length of interview

To make the informant feel comfortable, community researchers were encouraged to conduct the interview in an informal and as familiar a setting as possible. Most interviews took place in people's homes. The length of the interview varied depending upon the informant's interest and availability; the average session lasted about 1 hour. This was generally enough time to introduce most of the questionnaire topics; however, interviewers found that it was insufficient for in-depth discussion of important topics such as resource management. Also, there was little time to reflect on the discussion or to clarify any particular points without interrupting the flow of the interview. Community researchers recommended that in future projects, different subjects be covered over a series of interviews with one informant to allow the researcher time to evaluate the results before collecting more information.

## Group, pair, and individual interviews

Although the majority of interviews were conducted with one informant, some pair and group interviews were also tried. The research team found that group interviews tended to be confusing, both for the interviewer and informants, and almost impossible to control. Where several informants were involved, either the group tended to break into smaller discussion groups or one person tended to dominate the interview. Although it was not tried, the research team suggested that a group interview should concentrate on a few specific questions and should only be used to discuss and clarify variation in responses among different informants. This is one situation where the Steering Committee could have discussed specific topics and presented their decisions or results to the community researcher for the record.

## Recording information

All interviews were recorded on tape. Researchers were encouraged to take notes during the interview, writing down points and terminology for later clarification or for use in subsequent interviews. However, most single interviewers found it difficult to do this while keeping track of the questioning and encouraging the informant by expressing interest through eye contact and other responses. It was suggested that two researchers conduct the interview: one person concentrating on the interviewing and the other operating the tape recorder, taking notes, and interjecting questions where necessary.

Information about caribou migration routes and other habitat areas was also recorded on topographical maps when possible. Black-and-white and colour photographs were taken of different traditional activities by both outside researchers and local researchers throughout the year to use for displays and reports. Slides were also taken for future presentations.

## Guidelines for conducting interviews

From experience acquired during the pilot project, the research team compiled the following checklist of basic guidelines for conducting an interview.

1.  Meet with the informant to explain the goals of the project and what the informant can expect from the interview.

2.  Establish a convenient time and a quiet place to carry out the interview.

3.  Make sure that all equipment is in working order.

4.  Thoroughly review the questionnaire or checklist to ensure that you understand all of the topics being researched and the correct way to translate the questions into the Dene language.

5.  Before beginning the interview, put the informant at ease by making casual conversation and having tea together.

6.  Show the informant that you are interested in what he or she is saying. Use culturally appropriate interjections and gestures during the interview to encourage the informant to continue, expand, and provide details.

7.  Do not prompt the informant with an answer or ask leading questions.

8.  Use as many local examples as possible to explain your question to make sure the informant understands.

9.  Try to keep the flow of the interview as natural as possible. Allow the informant the freedom to talk about what he or she thinks is important without letting the informant wander away from the subject.

10. Don't pressure people to give specific numbers of animals regarding harvesting if they seem reluctant.

11. Encourage informants to record appropriate information on maps.

12. Be sensitive to fatigue or boredom of the informant. Encourage the informant to talk as long as possible; however, if the informant is tired or distracted, arrange to continue the interview at another time.

13. Maintain a sense of humour and never contradict or argue with an informant.

## Translation and transcription of interviews

The community researchers translated and transcribed the interviews into English to obtain the information necessary to answer the research questions. Eventually, when funds become available, the tapes will be transcribed into North Slavey. Translating the tapes directly into English created a number of problems. For the most part, researchers translated and transcribed without assistance. This was difficult for those who were not fluent in North Slavey or did not fully understand all of the concepts expressed by the informant in an older form of the language for which there was no literal translation into English.

It was generally believed that this information might be retrieved by someone who was not only fluent in the older language but also understood the appropriate method to discuss certain subjects. If the interviewer does not possess all of these skills, an elder, assisted by an interpreter who is fluent in English, would be a valuable asset for transcribing taped interviews.

Not enough time was devoted to deciphering the true meaning of Dene terms and concepts before determining if there was an equivalent term existing in the scientific terminology. In comparing terminology among different languages and cultures, there may be some terms and concepts that have a one-to-one correspondence in both languages; however, there may also be some that do not exist in the other language or that have a slightly different meaning.

## Data analysis and management

One of the objectives of the pilot project was to design a data-management system to handle the collected information. The Research Director did some preliminary investigation of different Geographical Information Systems (GIS) and other data base programs to determine their suitability to store and retrieve traditional knowledge. However, no firm decision concerning a suitable data-management system could be made until the data were collected or until there was a clear idea of how the data would be used in the community (for environmental management or educational purposes). For the moment, the data for the pilot project remains stored on tapes, in the English transcripts, and in the data summaries. Data from the transcripts were classified for each species according to the different subjects more or less as outlined in the questionnaire and summarized in nontechnical English.

## Dissemination of information

For TEK to gain acceptance among the younger generation of the Dene and for it to be recognized as a viable component of modern resource management, it must be documented and disseminated in a manner that is both meaningful and useful to appropriate audiences. To achieve this, the Dene Cultural Institute has, over the past 2 years, established cooperative working relationships with other agencies, both governmental and nongovernmental, involved in the documentation and application of traditional knowledge at local, territorial, national, and international levels. Plans are under way to publish a summary of the final report of the pilot project in the five Dene languages and distribute it to the different Dene communities. As well, papers discussing methodology and the preliminary results of the project will be submitted to various social science and environmental journals for publication.

# Preliminary Results: The Nature of Dene Traditional Environmental Knowledge

Like the traditional environmental knowledge of many indigenous peoples around the world, that of the Dene is a complex system that has been evolving since time immemorial. Although information gathered from this pilot project is preliminary, it clearly demonstrates that traditional environmental knowledge consists of a detailed knowledge of all the components of the natural environment and the practical and spiritual relationships of the Dene to these components. The traditional environmental knowledge of the Dene combines ecology and ideology in a harmonious relationship.

Most of the information collected focused on animal ecology. Specific ecological and biological information included descriptions of seasonal habitats of moose, caribou, beaver, and marten; foods and unique feeding habits (such as beaver and marten food caches); interspecific relationships (including predation, competition, and interdependence of different species such as beaver, muskrat, and water fowl); life histories; migrations and movements; and responses of animals to habitat alteration (fire, beaver pond draining, and oil-exploration roads, for example). Population cycles among traditionally cyclic varying hare and lynx and fluctuations in marten, moose, and caribou populations were commonly acknowledged, although the causes and specific time spans were seldom stated. Fisheries information mainly concerned spawning habits and seasonal movements of specific populations. Other mammals and birds were not part of the pilot project, although some incidental reference was made to them, particularly when discussing food habits and interspecific relationships. Although certain details of specific taxonomy and ecology were not obtained, the research team felt that these deficiencies were the result of the interview process (lack of time to ask probing questions, the unnatural setting, and inexperienced interviewers), not a lack of knowledge on the part of the informants. As previously noted, researchers often had difficulty interpreting Dene concepts into English scientific terminology.

It is still unclear to what extent Dene ideas about general ecosystems correspond to those of Western science. As demonstrated by their descriptions of animal habitat and interspecific relationships, many Dene understand complex ecological linkages. From a purely scientific perspective, the preliminary data reveal little that is not common knowledge among experienced ecologists, with some exceptions. However, it also appears that those Dene who have spent a large part of their life on the land possess as much understanding of wildlife and some fisheries ecology as many non-Dene scientists.

The observations made by Western scientists and Dene appear to differ in their emphasis; the two cultures look at different types of information to understand the environment. For example, not all hunters are familiar with certain minute details of moose habitat; however, they do know what is essential for moose at any given season, such as the required foods, escape cover, and terrain. An experienced hunter or ecologist looks at moose habitat in an holistic fashion in which the essentials stand out as "indicators" of habitat condition or habitat use. Inexperienced biologists and other outsiders tend to focus their entire attention on specific, isolated components of the ecosystem or animal populations. They often overlook less obvious factors or interrelationships that are critical to the survival and productivity of the population. For example, a biologist may see moose and an abundance of a preferred winter food species during a summer moose study and assume that it is excellent winter range. However, the Dene hunter/trapper knows the habits of moose and its use of habitat, sees no evidence of winter feeding (winter droppings, browsed twigs, etc.), and deduces that moose do not use the area in winter because of excessive snow depth, crusted snow, or some other factor.

One might assume from these preliminary observations, that Dene traditional knowledge is more utilitarian than esoteric in function. In other words, what people know is directly linked to their survival on the land. On a number of occasions, however, this assumption was challenged. In one instance, the research team listened to an elder explain in as much detail as any scientist the effects of permafrost and drainage on the composition and condition of two neighbouring plant communities. To what extent is this level of understanding of ecological processes not of direct utilitarian value present among other elders? This is currently unclear, but certainly merits further investigation. In any event, the range of quality in the information presented suggests that, as is common among any group of people, knowledge varies between individuals. Some people are naturally more curious and observant than others and, hence, will have a different level of understanding about certain phenomena.

Where Western science and Dene traditional knowledge diverge most notably is in their explanations of ecological processes and concepts of environmental management. For the traditional Dene, ideology is a fundamental element of subsistence, as important as practical empirical knowledge and appropriate technology. Traditional Dene ideology consists of a spiritually based moral code or ethic that governs the interaction between the human, natural, and spiritual worlds. It encompasses a number of general principles and specific rules that regulate human behaviour toward nature.

The fundamental principle of the traditional Dene environmental ideology is that the land and its resources should be tended for the benefit of future generations. Like other aboriginal cultures, the Dene view the Earth as a living organism. Animals, plants, humans, air, water, and land all have a reason for being and together maintain an intricate balance to ensure the continued survival of all life. Interference with any component of the environment, no matter how small, is bound to have negative repercussions on the other components. In many instances, there is reference to a higher power, the "Creator," who ensures that overall order is maintained in the system. Above all, humans do not have any special power or authority over other life-forms.

Spirituality is a pervasive dimension of the natural existence as it is perceived by the traditional Dene. Environmental events are believed to be caused or influenced by spiritual forces. Often these events are the result of some human action, especially a spiritual offense that alienates a part of the environment. The Dene conceptualize animals as social beings who communicate among themselves and understand human behaviour and language. Human qualities are often attributed to animals in many Dene legends. Specific rules that govern human behaviour toward natural entities include avoidance of waste (taking only what one needs), avoidance of live capture and captivity of animals, humane treatment of animals, use and respect for all parts of an animal, and respect for hunting and trapping equipment.

In addition to the general principles and specific rules developed to ensure the sustainable use of natural resources, the Dene have developed a number of harvesting strategies. All of these practices are based on an empirical understanding of population dynamics and ecological linkages. One strategy concerns the underuse and overuse of resources. Hunters believe that continued hunting and trapping of animals is important to achieve a sustainable, productive harvest, but that an area should also be allowed to rest for a period of time when a hunted species becomes scarce to let the population to renew itself. A second strategy involves the selective hunting of different sex and age-groups. For example, with beaver, the hunters usually take only mature animals and leave the mother during the spring, when she bears kits.

## Future Documentation

How traditional environmental knowledge will be used by future generations of Dene will vary according to the needs of different individuals and communities. Potential applications include the education of younger Dene and the development of a community-based system of resource management. Regardless of its eventual application, it is essential that all information be recorded as quickly as possible while it is still available in the minds of those who possess it. Further, it is important that the documented TEK be disseminated and actively used by people. Otherwise, it is liable to become little more than an intellectual curiosity relegated to the shelves of a museum or archive.

There are many worthwhile avenues of traditional environmental knowledge to pursue; ultimately, however, it should be up to the community involved to decide what information should be collected and how it should be applied. Some of the important subject areas and issues that may be part of future research in Fort Good Hope, Colville Lake, and other regions of Denendeh include

- Biological and ecological knowledge of all species of wildlife and fish that are of importance, utilitarian or otherwise, to the Dene residents of the region;

- Practical knowledge needed to hunt, trap, and fish successfully, including the many "indicators" used by experienced Dene to evaluate environmental conditions;

- A history of environmental changes in specific areas and the use of these areas by affected wildlife and fish species;

- The traditional Dene system of resource management, including the stories and legends that explain the Dene view of reality and rules regarding allocation and access to resources; and

- The impact of Euro-Canadian culture on the traditional management system to promote a better understanding of how Dene TEK and management practices have responded to changing technological, economic, political, and sociocultural conditions and how these factors have affected the ability of Dene to survive and adapt to new circumstances.

## Summary and Conclusions

One of the most important findings of the pilot project was the recognition of the difficulty and complexity of documenting and interpreting traditional environmental knowledge. From a methodological standpoint, it was difficult to design a method that could be applied by all interviewers and informants for all topics of investigation. Nevertheless, recognizing the number of variables involved in gathering information — such as differences in interviewers' levels of expertise, the setting of the interview, and the personalities of interviewers and informants — was important for realizing the importance of flexibility and innovation to the research approach. The pilot project identified the structured conversational approach to interviewing, supplemented by participant observation, as the best method to document traditional environmental knowledge. It also identified avoidable pitfalls in the translation of different knowledge systems, culturally appropriate methods of eliciting information, and proper procedures for the conduct of participatory community research in a Dene community.

In terms of obtaining a preliminary understanding of Dene TEK and the systems of traditional management that governs their use, the research team was able to identify the important types of environmental knowledge possessed by the elders of the community and some of the practices and beliefs that are essential to the traditional system of management. Some preliminary insight was also gained into the similarities and differences between Dene traditional knowledge and Western science. Although the pilot project did not reveal in a systematic way the extent to which the traditional system has been modified by Western culture or how it might best be integrated with Western science, it did raise important questions with which future research will have to deal.

The most important outcome of the pilot project in terms of active community involvement in research was the recognition that, for the most success, the initiative must come from the local people. The community must take responsibility for making decisions and assume responsibility for administering the project. Any other process that gives "outsiders" these responsibilities runs contrary to the goals of participatory community research and is unlikely to lead to a fully satisfactory conclusion.

# References

The Dene Nation. 1984. Denendeh: a Dene celebration. The Dene Nation, Yellowknife, NWT, Canada.

# Beaver Questionnaire

## Taxonomy (names for beaver)

1. Are there special Slavey names for different sexes and ages of beaver?
   (a) adult males (3 years or older)
   (b) adult females
   (c) 2- to 3-year-old males
   (d) 2- to 3-year-old females
   (e) 1- to 2-year-old males (yearlings)
   (f) 1- to 2-year-old females (yearlings)

2. Have you ever seen or heard about a black beaver or white (albino) beaver?

## Habitat and habitat relationships

1. Can you tell me about beaver habitat around lakes in summer?
   (a) type of environment
      – water depth
      – aquatic plants
      – terrestrial plants
      – exposure
      – type of soil
      – food plants used in summer
   (b) dwellings
      – types of dwellings (lodge, bank runs, bank dens)
      – materials used
      – location and exposure to sun and wind
      – size of dwellings
      – use of dwellings
   (c) beaver dams on lakes
      – location
      – materials used
      – when (before or after building lodge)

– effects of permafrost on location of lodge or run and
materials used

2.  Can you tell me about stream habitat in summer?
    (a) type of environment
       – water depth
       – speed of current
       – terrestrial plants used for foods
       – type of soil in banks and stream bed
    (b) dwellings
       – kinds of dwelling and use of them
       – where they are located
       – materials used
       – type of soil
       – effect of permafrost on location of dwellings and
         materials used
    (c) dams
       – location
       – materials used
       – method of construction
       – time of construction, before or after construction of
         dwelling
       – how dam is used to control water level
    (d) scent mounds
       – what they are and how they are used by beaver
       – when they are built

## Winter feeding habits

3.  Can you tell me about beaver winter feeding habits?
       – winter foods
       – storage of food in caches; where, when, and how food
         is stored
       – where food is eaten in winter
       – what beaver do if there is not enough food in winter
         caches

## *How beaver affect the environment*

4. Can you tell me how beaver affect the environment?
    - creation of new ponds or lakes in areas without permafrost
    - creation of new ponds or lakes in permafrost areas
    - changes in kinds of aquatic and terrestrial plants
    - damage done by beaver
    - change in habitat when all the beaver abandon (leave) an area or are killed off

## *Interspecific relationships*

1. Can you tell me about other wildlife and fish that share beaver habitat?
    - kinds of mammals, birds, and fish
    - animals that compete for food
    - predators of beaver and how they do it
    - animals that use beaver lodges and other dwellings

## *Life cycle, reproduction, and population dynamics*

1. Can you tell me about beaver mating habits and production of young?
    - time of year when mating occurs with evidence of mating
    - time of year when kits are born
    - normal number of kits
    - unusual high numbers of kits you have seen
    - what newborn beaver look like
    - length of nursing period
    - sex ratio of kits

2. Can you tell me other things about beaver populations?
    - how long young beaver live with their parents
    - number of beaver in winter lodges
    - ages of beaver in a lodge
    - estimating number of beaver in a lodge without

trapping the beaver
- summer movements of beaver (do they travel?)

3. Do you think beaver "families" have their own territories? If yes, what would you use as evidence of this?

4. Have you ever seen a time when beaver were scarce? If so, what do you think was the cause?

## Parasites and disease

1. Have you ever found dead beaver? If yes, do you know what was wrong with them?

2. What kind of external parasites (beetles, lice, fleas, or ticks) have you found on beaver? What did they look like?

3. Have you ever found signs of infection or parasites inside beaver? If yes, in what part of the animal (liver, spleen, lungs, etc.) and what did it look like?

4. Have you ever seen or heard of a beaver epidemic or a die-off as a result?

## Beaver trapping and management

### Traditional

1. Can you tell me how Dene caught beaver before steel traps and wire snares?

2. Can you tell me about the traditional laws or rules for hunting beaver?
	- what people did to make sure that there would always be beaver for future generations
	- limits placed on numbers, sex, or age of beaver hunted and how this was accomplished
	- how to show respect for beaver

### Modern

1. Can you tell me about modern trapping methods?
	- the best size leg-hold trap for catching beaver

   – how to set traps in open water
   – how to set traps under ice

2.  Do you use Connibear (square) traps for beaver?
    – when to use them: under ice or open water or both
    – how and where to set them in open water
    – how to set Connibear traps under ice
    – what is good/bad about the Connibear trap for beaver
    – when you hunt beaver (what months?)
    – why you hunt beaver then

3.  How do you know how may beaver you can take without hurting the rest of the population?

4.  Do you have special areas where you hunt beaver?
    – reasons for hunting there
    – number of years you have been hunting there

5.  Do other people have special areas where they hunt beaver like you do?

6.  If *you* were the game warden in charge of beaver management, what rules would you make to ensure that beaver are used wisely?
    – limits or quotas
    – seasons for trapping
    – other rules (laws)
    – estimates of population
    – use of traditional laws to improve modern management

# Reindeer Management in Canada's Belcher Islands: Documenting and Using Traditional Environmental Knowledge

The Belcher Island Adaptive Reindeer Management Project is a collaborative, community-based research initiative involving the Inuit community of Sanikiluaq and the Canadian Circumpolar Institute (CCI) in Edmonton, Alberta. The project promotes a mutual exchange of information between scientists and Inuit hunters concerning population, habitat status, and management needs for a population of reindeer recently introduced to the Belcher Islands. Traditional environmental knowledge of the Belcher Island Inuit is integral to the project because of its important contribution to the wildlife-management and research process. This paper reviews some of the methods employed for documenting and using traditional environmental knowledge in cooperative environmental management.

By Miriam McDonald Fleming, Belcher Island Adaptive Reindeer Management Project, Sanikiluaq, NWT, Canada (now with the Hudson Bay Program of the Canadian Arctic Resources Committee, the Environmental Committee of Sanikiluaq, and the Rawson Academy of Aquatic Science).

# The Belcher Islands and Its People

The Belcher Islands are situated in the southeastern portion of Hudson Bay, the largest inland sea in North America. They constitute a large, unique archipelago of about 1 500 islands encompassing an approximate area of 3 200 square kilometres (Fig. 1). The size of individual islands range from less than 1 square kilometre in the "offshore" islands to approximately 80 square kilometres in the "mainland" islands.

Geologically, the islands are low-lying Precambrian outcrops extending in a north–south direction. About 8 thousand years ago, the archipelago was covered by a thick layer of glacial ice. Global warming induced intensive glacial activity that aided in producing a treeless landscape characterized by smooth rock ridges, tundra vegetation, and inland lakes.

Winds have a strong modifying effect on climate and vegetation growth in the Belcher Islands. Prevailing northwest winds travel approximately 900 kilometres across Hudson Bay before sweeping over the islands. The air is cooled considerably and seasonal temperatures are significantly lower relative to continental localities at the same latitude.

By November, sea ice starts to form around the islands and, in recent years, has not completely left the area until August. The snow disappears in June and plants have adapted to a typically short, 3-month growing season. Arctic mosses, lichens, sedges, and some grasses are the predominant vegetation. The ground usually starts freezing again in October.

The community of Sanikiluaq is situated on the southeastern side of Eskimo Harbour (Fig. 1). It was established as a government service and administration centre in 1970, and is the most southern settlement in the Northwest Territories of Canada. The Inuit of Sanikiluaq are the only people to live year-round, on a permanent basis, in the archipelago. The population of

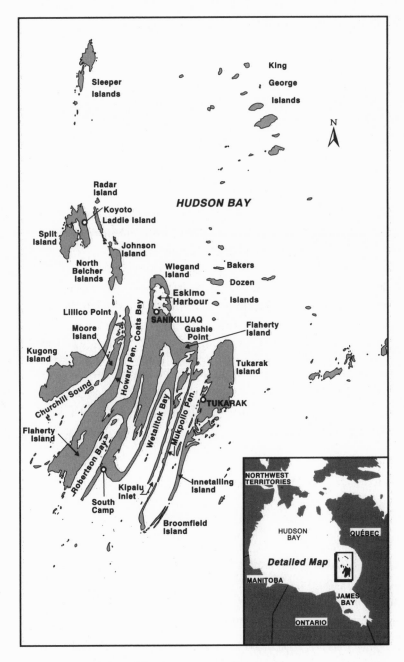

Fig. 1. *The Belcher Islands of Canada's Northwest Territories, site of the Adaptive Reindeer Management Project.*

Sanikiluaq is about 470 Inuit, along with 30 to 40 transient workers from the south.

Sea mammals, birds, sea ducks, fish, and reindeer are sustaining foods for Belcher Island Inuit. People eat in synchronization with the annual cycles of different animal, bird, and fish species. They enjoy a highly nourishing and, traditionally, low-disease diet. Because of climatic factors and low productivity in arctic terrestrial and marine environments, however, this diet is also susceptible to food shortages.

The people of Sanikiluaq, formerly known as *Qikitarmiut* ("People of the Islands"), travel extensively throughout the Belcher Islands. In spring, shortly after the geese return, many families return to live off the land until the sea ice deteriorates in late May. Following break-up of the sea ice in late June, families resume traveling and living throughout the archipelago until late August when school commences. During early fall and winter, men travel hundreds of kilometres throughout the islands to hunt and fish.

Through the course and in the tradition of arctic living, Belcher Island Inuit have acquired a rich and diverse knowledge of the natural world in which they live and that they share with other living beings.

## *The Adaptive Reindeer Management Project*

Reindeer are a terrestrial mammal and were brought to the Belcher Islands by the Government of the Northwest Territories in 1978. At the time, community and government people hoped the reindeer would adapt successfully to the Belcher Island environs and, thereby, supplement the traditional diet of predominantly marine foods.

Before reindeer were introduced, there was no large, land-based animal living in the islands; caribou, a species closely related to reindeer disappeared in the late 1800s. Inuit and scientists say freezing rain created a hard layer of ice that the caribou could not penetrate for feeding (Elton 1942). Unable to access grazing grounds, the caribou left the islands and never returned (Anonymous 1982). A hundred years later, the reindeer entered a rich, undisturbed habitat. To date, they have adapted well and the population is growing rapidly. They have become a new food resource valued and cared for by the community.

For the first years, the reindeer were left alone to establish themselves in the Islands. They spread throughout the Islands, south of Sanikiluaq, until a main herd moved into the southwestern region of Flaherty Island. By 1982, the population had grown large enough to sustain the first community harvest. Every household enjoyed a share of the return.

As community harvests continued, originally on an annual and then seasonal basis, the hunters interacted increasingly with the reindeer. They also began noticing how fast the population was growing. The birth of twins was common, and some reindeer bore triplets. Harvesting effort was increasing, and the population was growing quickly (Arragutainaq et al. 1990).

The Belcher Island Adaptive Reindeer Management Project originated in 1987 when CCI responded to interest on the part of the community to learn more about, and to care for, the introduced reindeer species. Based on the observation that reindeer seemed to multiply quickly in a short period of time, community hunters had many questions about rate of reproduction, herd formations, breeding cycles, and feeding areas. Essentially, they wanted to study the reindeer; but, living in today's world and not being scientists, they needed assistance in accessing funding and initiating a community-based study.

Researchers at CCI were interested in working with the community because it was apparent the people were asking questions of legitimate scientific and wildlife-management concern. It was also apparent that although Sanikiluaq residents professed to be learning about the reindeer, they already held considerable knowledge of the reindeer's niche in the Belcher Islands.

Hence, the project adopted three principal objectives:

- To answer the management-oriented questions raised by the community;

- To develop a wildlife-management system that incorporates the traditional environmental knowledge of Belcher Island Inuit and scientific techniques of wildlife biologists; and

- To develop a viable model for community-based management of wildlife resources in the Canadian North.

## *Inuit Environmental Knowledge in Arctic Wildlife Management*

Canadian government agencies and cooperative management boards are assuming an increasingly active role in managing arctic wildlife species. This is occurring in convergence with the imminent settlement of aboriginal land claims, deterioration of the arctic marine habitat, and recognition of the importance of wildlife to sustaining life in the arctic (Freeman 1988).

Under these circumstances, the contribution of original peoples' knowledge to wildlife-management and research processes is invaluable. These people live in direct contact with the animal, bird, and fish species. Moreover, they benefit from generations of knowledge and experience in living in the arctic environment. As such, they have the empirical knowledge to address key principles in the wildlife-management process, at a time when scientific information on many species and most populations remains limited and fragmented.

Generations of experience with wildlife has enabled Inuit hunters to understand fluctuations within annual and other cycles of arctic animal populations. They also understand that among the various causes of mortality within those cycles there is a pervasive relationship: if one thing does not "get them" something else will. This was evident when discussing community management of the Hudson Bay eider duck with Belcher Island Inuit. In developing a community-based management strategy, the people considered levels of impact from their own use as well as impacts related to weather, the sea ice environment, and at least four other species (Municipality of Sanikiluaq 1990a).

In the arctic, population levels shift constantly and the environment alters continuously with the cycle of seasons. Thus, an Inuk hunter tends not to think in absolute terms but, rather, in terms of ecological relationships that emphasize cyclical trends influencing wildlife populations. Indeed, a major theme emerging from this research is the need for arctic wildlife management to assume a broader ecological perspective.

As a means of demonstrating the nature and importance of Inuit ecological thinking, and in light of its relevancy to documenting traditional environmental knowledge, a lengthy, though abridged, excerpt from a taped interview is presented:

*Respondent*: If you were really talking with somebody, like an older person about the snow, because there's no words in English, it is called white, brown, black. But there's actually more names than just black and brown for snow.

*Interviewer*: That's what I was wondering. Are there terms for the different layers of snow?

*Respondent*: Yes, because the layers are actually coming in different times. In the fall, the snow comes, then later on it builds up and it looks different.

*Interviewer*: So, are there layers of hard snow then light snow?

*Respondent*: Not of hard snow. Because the bottom part, the first snow that falls, becomes crystal snow when the newer snows build up on top of it. Crystal snow is like those small ice crystals. The bottom snow turns into that.

*Interviewer*: Would the other snow on top also turn into crystals?

*Respondent*: No. Only the lower snow, the lowest one, becomes crystals. Even in the winter time.

*Interviewer*: How?

*Respondent*: I don't know. Maybe it's because it comes in as a hard, packed snow at first but as the snow builds up on top of it, not enough air is coming out. But, when the weather becomes mild, during the winter time, it's warmer down there, and that's why it becomes crystal snow.

*Interviewer*: So, is that the snow that the reindeer can't get through?

*Respondent*: No, not that one. The snow the reindeers won't be able to get into is the first snow that becomes really solid.

Any day now the ground is going to start freezing. During this time we're going to get falling snow. A few inches is going to build up, but later on we're going to be hit by mild weather, really, really mild weather. It's actually going to melt the snow. There will be water build up on top of the ground because the snow that was already there will be melting. It will turn into ice, solid ice. Maybe that will be the hardest part to get into, by the reindeer.

*Interviewer*: You're trying to find out about snow?

*Respondent*: Yes, and how reindeer feed in the winter.

Up here, snow is really in the barren land. There's no willow trees or anything to stop the snow from blowing out. It's always blowing in the winter time so it makes very hard-packed snow. Very hard, almost as hard as rock sometimes. It is snow hardened by the wind.

*Interviewer*: Would reindeer be able to get through that snow?

*Respondent*: Yes. I think they can get through that snow because it's not really, really solid ice. It is hard, but it can be scraped by the reindeer. It is that early snow, the one that comes in early and thaws out in the early fall or early winter that you have to worry about for the reindeer. Because it will thaw out, and when it freezes again, it becomes solid ice.

*Interviewer*: So, that's a critical time for the reindeer?

*Respondent*: Maybe, because the early snow that melts is going to be covered with new snow and it's going to be frozen solid down there. And, when the reindeer paw through that snow they are going to hit that very hard part. But it's not going to cover the whole island. Okay? It's only going to cover so much of the ground.

Because it's early winter, we're going to have only a small layer of snow on the ground and there won't be enough snow yet to cover the whole island. That snow will melt and then freeze into ice but there won't be enough snow yet to cover the whole island.

Just the lower parts in the land will be covered with a small amount, maybe a few inches, of snow. That part is what you have to be worried about.

But you can't really worry about reindeers not being able to get to the feeding ground. If it rains in early winter, November, there will not be not enough snow over the islands. But if we get actual rain in December, when there is more snow, then you will get worried about reindeers not being able to get to the food.

*Interviewer:* Because when it rains then it would cover everything?

*Respondent:* Yes, it will. Anything that was there is going to freeze, including the feed. The vegetation will actually be frozen because of the rain. But if we have a regular season and no rain in December but just more and more snow, you don't have to worry about the reindeers.

*Interviewer:* Is that more likely to happen on a year like this, when the snow is late?

*Respondent:* No. It never fails. It always comes. Whether you like it or not, the mild, mild weather will be here. But you can never tell exactly when. It will be here the last few days of October, or very early November. If it doesn't happen then, it's coming in later. It even happens in December. But, if it's not here in early November, it's not normal and it's going to affect the whole weather system.

If the milder weather comes in December, it actually melts and within a few days its going to be cold, very, very cold. Much colder weather will hit after it melts.

*Interviewer:* Why is that?

*Respondent:* I don't know. It always has been like that. You can't really explain it, but if you were to ask people, the older people, they know, but they don't really have the explanation for it. They just know it's going to affect the weather. Okay?

Just like last winter, we had the really mild weather in late March. We actually had rain in March and the snow melted. It was like springtime, but it came too early. When that happened, then you got to be hit by very long, cold weather in later months. Like we had, this spring. Most of May was frozen but it was supposed to be melting.

*Interviewer:* What happens when it melts in March?

*Respondent:* When it melts in March, it freezes over. The whole ground freezes over so it could have been a few inches of solid ice built up right over the whole island.

*Interviewer:* Because when it melts it is melting into the snow?

*Respondent:* Yes. When it melts, it drains out through the snow so whatever is below freezes into ice. At that time, then you will be thinking about the reindeers not being able to get to the feeding ground. Because it's too early for the snow to be melting.

March is not thawing time. Normally in March, the weather is starting to get a little bit better but it's not going to start melting. But the one we had last year, it was melting because it was raining. The weather was warmer for a day, maybe two days that's it. Then it got back to normal weather, which is 20 degrees [Celsius] below zero.

*Interviewer:* So, if I understand right, it is not difficult for the reindeer to get through hard snow.

*Respondent:* No, it's not a problem. They can still get through it. They will scrape it with their hooves. Just like they do in the wintertime. They have to, to get to the feeding. *Ajjaatuk* means getting the snow off the ground.

But, in case of very mild days during the winter, you have to worry about them because then the snow will turn into ice, solid ice if it melted. If not, nothing to worry about.

# Documenting Traditional Environmental Knowledge

The primary purpose in documenting traditional environmental knowledge in the case of the Adaptive Reindeer Management Project is to that ensure as complete a body of knowledge as possible is available for decision-making. It complements the biological, population, and habitat data that are being collected and analyzed by standard scientific procedures. The other main purpose is to demonstrate the nature and extent of Inuit environmental knowledge to the larger wildlife-management community, public policymakers in the Canadian North, scientists involved in the project, and, to some degree, the Inuit themselves. It is challenging because of the interaction between different world views, differing ways of knowing, and the fact that the idea of traditional environmental knowledge is as new to scientists as the Western concept of wildlife management is to Belcher Island Inuit.

The process of documenting traditional environmental knowledge has evolved, and continues to evolve, into a methodology. From the onset, it has been a highly adaptive process guided by principles that are both closely associated with the opportunity to learn about the natural world in which the Belcher Island Inuit live and grounded in respect for Inuit and the knowledge they have developed to live in the arctic environment.

The different settings in which knowledge has been shared and exchanged include camp situations, hunting trips, community committee meetings, casual conversations, informal discussions, and formal interviews. Active participation in each setting has been essential as, collectively, they provide a broad and diverse range of experiences in which the nature of Inuit environmental knowledge can be understood and documented.

The research began in 1988. At that time, the intent was seemingly simple: to learn what the people knew about reindeer. This approach provided me with opportunities to spend considerable time with people living off the land during spring and summer months and to participate in community reindeer hunts during the summer and winter periods. The experiences from these opportunities were valuable because they built an appreciation for how reindeer fit into the Belcher Inuit way of life. In turn, I recognized the opportunity to learn a way of life and manner of relating to the natural world completely different from my own past experience. I also began to recognize the kinds of knowledge required to lead a subsistence life in the Belcher Islands, particularly with regard to successful procurement, preparation, and distribution of wild foods.

The learning process, however, was influenced by my inability to speak and understand Inuktitut and the Belcher Island dialect. In camp and on hunting trips, dialogue was restricted to very basic Inuktitut. Communication itself came from the freedom to participate and people showing me how to perform certain tasks associated with subsistence life. It often seemed intrusive and inappropriate to speak in English even when there was opportunity. Also, most of the time, it never occurred to me, as I was fully occupied keeping pace with surrounding events and activities.

In the community, conversations happened more spontaneously in light of seasonal events in the natural world, shared observations, and hunting activities. At these times, people spoke freely in terms of what they know because I was trying to understand the world in which I was now living. Sometimes, the conversations evolved into actual lessons on interpretation and practical use of particular natural phenomena. On other occasions, discussions focused on concepts and their relevance to wildlife management, research, and different ways of knowing. The spontaneity of these conversations rendered them impossible to record on tape. They were, however, recorded in a journal for the insight they provide into understanding the traditional environmental knowledge of Belcher Island Inuit.

*Thursday, 30 March 1989*

S. was saying E. is good at navigating by natural signs, sun, waves, currents, when traveling in sea water without land in sight. In these times, the wind doesn't help very much because it is always going around, never staying in one place. You can't really navigate by wind in any season he says. People can navigate by the sun and waves though. If it is cloudy, people will navigate by the waves.

Birds and ducks are also used for navigation. If a bird or duck is seen and it is flying in one direction then it is going towards land, i.e., *takatakiak, nirliit, mitiit. Takatakiak* can be flying quite a distance from the land "because those small birds are always eating." If in a thick fog on a calm day, you can listen for the songs of birds and, also, the sound of waves washing up on the shore. Those sounds can direct you toward land.

On one occasion, someone asked S. about management long ago. S. said he didn't really know what to say other than people only hunted what they needed and never took more than they needed over a 2- to 3-day period.

I suggested if you wanted to understand management you would need to look at use over time and through the seasons. S. then spoke with respect to two species: eider ducks and geese.... As we ended, he commented "even though we've been managing the animals we haven't known it because it is just what we do."

During the conversation, S. also gave a very interesting description of the "bubbles" eider ducks form amongst the sea ice during winter.

In 1988, 1989, and much of 1990, the focus of inquiry was not limited to reindeer. There were several reasons for this, including the people's inclination to talk of other species and the world they share with those species. Also, I was involved with the Sanikiluaq Hunters' and Trappers' Association (HTA) in developing a community-based management strategy for commercial use of eider down from the eider duck population (Municipality of Sanikiluaq 1990a). Numerous committee meetings afforded the opportunity to learn about and document traditional environmental knowledge of the Belcher Island Inuit. Extensive notes were recorded during these meetings so that the insight, observations, perspectives, and beliefs of people could be studied and considered for the management strategy. As a community-based strategy, consistency with the beliefs, values, and practices of people using the resource was essential to ensure implementation.

Translation was essential in meetings, and the role of translators was critical to two-way communication. As the following passage attests, it was also a forum in which I began learning the importance of asking questions in a language that could be translated and understood.

*April 1989*

In the HTA meeting I asked two questions, but didn't get too far. The first question was, "What are the key changes within the eider population that serve as response indicators to management activities?"

The response was, "This is a hard question to ask because we don't think of these things from a monitoring point of view. We just do it."

The second question was related to scientific concern with numbers when it comes to managing animals. When F. was here, he suggested one monitoring procedure could be to count all the nests on every second island from which down is collected. This way the number of nests could be monitored in terms of going up and down over time. So, I asked whether this is practical or if there are more effective ways of monitoring changes in the eiders?

The response was, "There may be lots of nests first year. The next year there may be nothing because of foxes. Year after, the eiders might return. After the foxes leave. There is one island where there were lots of nests. Last year there was nothing because there were cubs and foxes there."

In 1990, each of the settings discussed for documenting traditional environmental knowledge remain applicable whenever the appropriate opportunity arises. However, it became apparent that, for the purposes of the Adaptive Reindeer Management Project, I needed to talk with individuals directly about the reindeer. As such, many problems arose: language, content, translation, time. People, men and women, were readily identified; but, to engage their cooperation, the interviewing experience must be meaningful and of relevance to them.

The interviewing process is currently underway and five interviews have been conducted to date. They range in duration from less than a minute to just over 3 hours. Three of the interviews were recorded on tape. The fourth person preferred not to use the tape recorder. The fifth interview consisted of two sentences: "I don't have anything to say about those reindeer. They're still a mystery to me." With one exception, the interviews have been conducted in English; the remaining sessions will require an interpreter. A single interview has been transcribed, producing a 56-page transcript.

Considerable time went into preparing for the interviews. Nine main areas of inquiry were identified and organized into specific topics of discussion: seasonal observations, seasonal movements, population dynamics, foraging behaviour, interspecies interactions, historical characteristics, environmental factors, Inuit terminologies, and human use. Before an interview, I set objectives with regard to the specific areas of inquiry I intended to discuss. These objectives have proven invaluable in focusing the discussions; however, the course taken in an actual interview is determined in cooperation with the person being interviewed.

The greatest challenges in conducting the interviews have been to "break the ice," so that everyone feels comfortable, and to create an atmosphere in which knowledge can be shared. In one interview, these obstacles were overcome once we began discussing a community reindeer hunt we had participated in the previous winter. From there, we moved onto a time when the person was sitting on his snow machine watching reindeer. The observations the respondent shared about patterns of leadership within the herd are valuable to addressing the potential issue of encouraging the reindeer to move out of a heavily grazed area. They help in learning how traditional environmental knowledge is acquired. And, moreover, I learned that it is essential to develop the experiential basis from which an individual can relate and respond. Otherwise, the individual is uncertain of how to answer questions and share his or her knowledge.

## Project Administration

The Belcher Island Adaptive Reindeer Management Project is administered by the Hunters' and Trappers' Association (HTA) in cooperation with project researchers from CCI and a consultant. The documentation of traditional environmental knowledge is one aspect of this larger project.

The project has a research coordinator, based at CCI, who identifies potential funding sources and people with the relevant expertise to become involved in the project. HTA's Secretary-Treasurer is the project's community coordinator. He manages project funds, as they are received, and is the researchers' principal contact in the community. He is also the liaison between a federal government agency, a territorial government agency, CCI, and HTA. The project researchers assist in preparing funding proposals for approval and submission by HTA. They also conduct research in the areas of population status, habitat condition, and traditional environmental knowledge.

## Reporting and Data Management

Annual workshops are integral to the project. The workshops are held in the community to review research results, identify problems, and set directions for the upcoming year. In the first year, the hunters designed a cost-effective way of ground surveying the reindeer population based on experiential knowledge and the use of appropriate technology and methods (Arragutainaq et al.

1989). Their methodology was validated through use in conjunction with aerial surveys for 2 years (Arragutainaq et al. 1990). This year, the ground survey will be used exclusive of an aerial survey. It is also being replicated to estimate the number of caribou on Banks Island in the western Canadian arctic (Anonymous 1990).

Also this year, the people's knowledge of reindeer ecology will be organized into a written format and presented to workshop participants. It is being prepared so that Inuit environmental knowledge is systemically brought into the management process and is used in considering research and management priorities in the upcoming year. The presentation will be augmented by the knowledge HTA and community members bring forward in the workshop.

The notes that have been recorded since 1988 are currently being organized by season and harvesting activity in terms of knowledge required and generated. They will form a working paper to guide further research into the Belcher Island Inuit's knowledge of the Hudson Bay ecological system.

The taped interviews are being transcribed. Copies of the transcripts will be given to each interviewee and to HTA. Although the transcripts will be in English, it is important that the people interviewed receive a copy. They will then see an outcome of the interviewing process.

## *Outcomes and Consequences*

At all levels and stages of this project, it has been critical to develop and maintain the research in a context that supports the expression of peoples' views and the knowledge they have acquired from interacting with the reindeer and the natural world. Since preliminary discussions, Belcher Island Inuit have emphasized they are "still learning about reindeer" for two reasons. First, direct experience with the *Rangifer* species was limited until introduction of reindeer in 1978. Second, irrespective of expertise, Belcher Island Inuit wonder and are cautious about communicating their knowledge to the Western world. By nature, they are more inclined to ask questions that "press for proper answers to fundamental environmental, human health [and management] questions" (Gamble 1990, p. 11; Municipality of Sanikiluaq 1990b). They support processes that seek to answer those questions and have a valuable role, themselves, in addressing the ecologically based questions they pose. We hope initiatives like the Fort Good Hope Workshop help to develop such processes, for the benefit of indigenous peoples, Western society, and the global environment.

## *References*

Anonymous. 1982. Reindeer transplanted to Belcher Islands 100 years after native caribou disappears. Caribou News, 1982. p. 11

Anonymous. 1990. Caribou shortage means quota for Sachs Harbour. The Press Independent, 20(32), 3.

Arragutainaq, L., Hudson, R.J., Poole, P. 1989. Winter reindeer survey on the Belcher Islands, 1989. Department of Indian and Northern Affairs, Ottawa, Ont., Canada.

_____1990. Reindeer surveys on the Belcher Islands, 1989-90. Weasels Hunters' and Trappers' Association, Sanikiluaq, NWT, Canada.

Elton, C. 1942. Voles, mice and lemmings: problems in population dynamics. Clarendon Press, Oxford, UK. pp. 366–367.

Freeman, M.M.R. 1988. Environment, society and health: quality of life issues in the contemporary north. Arctic Medical Research, 47(Suppl. 1), 53–59.

Gamble, D. 1990. Groping around James Bay, federal myopia or intentional blindness? Arctic Circle, 1990(Nov./Dec.), 10–11.

Municipality of Sanikiluaq. 1990a. Development of community-based eider down industry in Sanikiluaq: resource management and business strategies. A report prepared for the Canada–NWT Economic

Development Agreement. Community Economic Development, Municipality of Sanikiluaq, NWT, Canada. 48 pp.

_____1990b. Environmental concerns of Sanikiluaq residents for Phase II of James Bay Hydro-Electricity Project. Environmental Committee, Sanikiluaq, NWT, Canada.

૨૭

# THE SOUTH PACIFIC

*The South Pacific is home to a myriad of island groups. One of these groups, the Solomon Islands, provides the setting for the following case study. The Marovo Lagoon Resource Management Project was initiated by the Marovo community of Western Province. The paper, by Graham Baines and Edvard Hviding, describes the reciprocal nature of the project's research. Visiting scientists impart their experience to Marovo residents. In turn, the Marovo people provide the visitors with hands-on training in traditional skills. The results are mutually beneficial and act to preserve the traditional wisdom of the Marovo community.*

# Traditional Environmental Knowledge from the Marovo Area of the Solomon Islands

The Solomon Islands is a country of many islands and large tracts of sea, neighbouring Papua New Guinea, about 3 hours flying time from Australia (Fig. 1). The Marovo area of Western Province, one of seven provinces of the Solomon Islands, is dominated by a large coastal lagoon embracing several high volcanic islands. This reef and lagoon complex skirts the northern and eastern coasts of New Georgia and Vangunu islands, covering an area of about 700 square kilometres. In the lagoon area and on the weather coasts of the main islands live some 8 000 people. These people form a cultural complex where the Marovo language is dominant, although four other languages are also indigenous to the area. The marine and terrestrial components of the environment are managed through a complex system of customary tenure where descent groups control ancestral territories of land, reef, and lagoon.

The main "high" islands of Marovo have a largely intact cover of tropical rain forest, only a few areas having been subject to commercial logging. The forest provides medicinal plants, housing materials, trees for dugout canoes, and animal protein (wild

By Graham Baines, Environment Pacific, Brisbane, Australia, and Edvard Hviding, Centre for Development Studies, University of Bergen, Bergen, Norway.

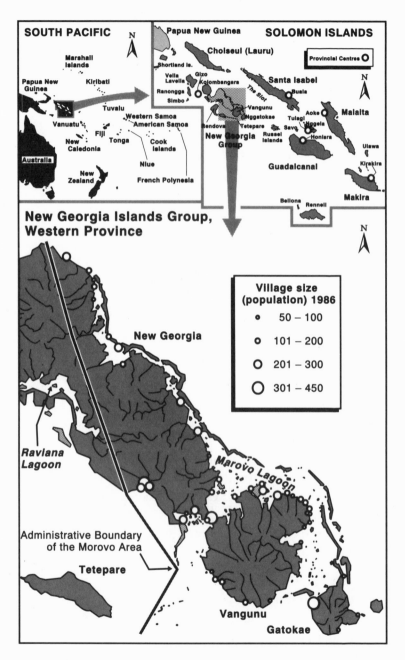

*Fig. 1. Islands of the South Pacific, the Solomon Islands, and the New Georgia Island Group of Western Province, showing the location of Marovo Lagoon and the Marovo area.*

pig, possum, and birds, among others). Subsistence agriculture is carried out on the lower slopes. Commercial crops of cocoa and coconut are also grown, the latter occupying much of the small area of flat coastal land.

The lagoon is studded with a myriad of small islands, many of which are covered with forest and fringed with mangroves; others are planted with coconuts. The barrier reef extends around a series of forested, raised fossil reef islands, intersected by passages. The complex reef environment surrounding the barrier islands contains Marovo's most important fishing grounds. A vast variety of fish, shellfish, molluscs, and crustaceans (as well as declining populations of turtles and dugong) is available at the barrier reef, in the lagoon, and in the extensive mangrove areas along mainland coasts. Marine resources also include commercial stocks of pearl shell, trochus, bêche-de-mer, and precious coral. The barrier islands also supply certain valuable resources that are now becoming jealously guarded, such as "Kerosene wood" for carving and coconut crabs.

The environment of Marovo has been little disturbed by human activity, and many areas still have a near-pristine quality. The Marovo people have access to a diverse and rich supply of natural resources. However, prospects of further rapid population growth and an expected increase in commercial ventures of fishing, mining, logging, and tourism pose difficulties for Marovo community hopes of maintaining the current quality of resources and environment.

## The Marovo Lagoon Resource Management Project

"The Marovo Project" was initiated in December 1985 with the first Marovo Community Workshop, held at the administrative centre of Seghe. Although provided with some government guidance in its early stages, the Marovo Project is essentially a community activity arising from an initiative of the Marovo community itself — through the Marovo Area Council — and with the active support of the government of Western Province.

The objectives of the Marovo Project are

- To define and describe the resources and environment of the Marovo lagoon and its islands, with particular reference to their close association with Marovo society;

- To describe and explain the various development activities underway and proposed, their benefits and shortcomings, and their environmental and social consequences;

- To assist the development of a local community capacity to assess, monitor, and sustainably use the resources of the people of Marovo;

- Building on traditional arrangements, to assist landholding groups to devise management plans for their land and lagoon areas;

- Through a focus on environment and resource use in relation to tradition and social and economic developmental needs, to foster the concept of "Marovo community";

- To encourage and support women to gain more recognition for their contribution to development and to assist them to further develop their understanding and skills in this area; and

- To offer knowledge and understanding gained from the project to other communities and agencies of the Solomon Islands and the South Pacific Island region.

It is clear, then, that the Marovo Project did not arise specifically to document traditional environmental knowledge. This is, however, a vitally important element.

## Project perspectives

The Marovo people have a great pride in their lagoon and its surrounding rain forest islands. They are also immensely proud of the extent of their knowledge and understanding of the environment, which is the focus of their culture and livelihood. This is the background to a concern about ad hoc resource exploration and development in their area. In 1984, this concern led the Marovo Area Council to call for assistance that would lead to a more orderly examination of resource potential and to more involvement and a more informed choice of development options by the people of Marovo.

The first author of this paper, while Senior Planning Officer with the government of Western Province, was allocated the task of sifting through the ideas and information provided through the Marovo Area Council and of working with the people of Marovo to establish a project framework. He was also called upon to advise on how scientific or technical expertise could be applied to expressed Marovo needs in natural resource management. With the assistance of the London-based Commonwealth Science Council, the Marovo Lagoon Resource Management Project was subsequently established as a community-based program of activities with carefully chosen outside interventions in the form of "visiting investigators" invited to apply their skills and knowledge in ways relevant to the Project.

Key features of the Project's approach to documenting traditional environmental knowledge include

- A strong emphasis on partnerships between Marovo informants and investigators, whether local or visiting;

- A process of information exchange rather than formal interviewing;

- Visiting investigators learning traditional skills and information by doing; and

❧ Promoting feedback of traditional environmental knowledge in documented form to sustain and stimulate the interest of informants and to make others more quickly aware of the nature and extent of the environmental knowledge that is part of Marovo culture.

The reporting element of the Marovo Project is crucial. Various procedures for reporting have been and are being tried. The main community focus for reporting has been a series of annual workshops. These workshops provide a forum to report the results obtained by visiting investigators, discuss future investigative work with community representatives, and generally debate development issues of immediate concern to the community. Of the 8 thousand people that make up the community of Marovo, 50 to 60 representatives participate in each workshop.

## Project administration

From December 1985 to May 1988, the Project was administered by an on-site Project Organizer working closely with a Research Organizer, who was affiliated with the Ministry of Natural Resources in the national capital of the Solomon Islands, Honiara. Their part-time assistance to the Project was funded by the Commonwealth Science Council. Additional support was provided by the administration of Western Province and by an unpaid informal support group of individuals resident at Gizo (the administrative centre of Western Province) and in Honiara. Project activities were organized in association with the local government administration, the Marovo Area Council. Research and surveys were undertaken by visiting investigators from local and overseas institutions. A total of 16 visiting investigators have been involved with the Project to date, in assignments varying in length from 1 week to 18 months.

The Research Organizer assists in identifying information needs, advising Project staff regarding suitable studies, and identifying investigators to undertake such studies. From the initial framework of research priorities established in 1985 at the first Marovo Community Workshop, many Project activities have been formulated. Generally, they fall into five main themes: coastal zone systems, society and resources, traditional knowledge, coastal resource assessment, and education and training. Overall responsibility for the continuous planning of activities rests with the Research Organizer, in close collaboration with local-level Project staff, the Marovo Project Support Group, and visiting investigators. The Support Group is now the administrative focus of the Project.

Many new priorities and Project activities have arisen spontaneously in the course of daily interaction between visiting investigators and the citizens of Marovo. In many cases, as general attention has focused on environmental knowledge, Marovo elders — senior men and women such as chiefs, local historians, and master fishers — have requested detailed documentation of a certain aspect of traditional knowledge that they feel is of particular importance. It has usually been possible for investigators to comply with such wishes, sometimes by bringing in outside expertise. For example, an experienced biologist well acquainted with spawning aggregations of coral reef fish was brought to Marovo. The biologist worked together with local experts to record the complex knowledge of Marovo fishers on such aggregations; a knowledge of which the local fishers are justifiably proud (see Johannes 1988).

On-site research has been characterized by a loosely formulated structure of "informal" research administration. Elders, local Project staff, interviewers, interpreters, and other villagers guide the visiting investigator to the topics and locations deemed to be particularly relevant. In the case of the spawning coral reef fish, the biologist was taken to several spawning grounds during various phases of the moon in accordance with the rhythms followed by the Marovo fishers. The research design was adapted as new findings emerged and lessons were learned. In those Marovo villages that have been most closely involved in Project research, there is an established emphasis on "taking charge": organizing the working day of the visiting investigator and so influencing the research process. This is seen as a way of ensuring that the investigator receives his or her education in the soundest and most detailed manner possible. A researcher is often sent on to other villages to visit resident experts to obtain "the truth" about certain areas of environmental knowledge.

A wealth of information about Marovo, its people, and its resources has been documented in the course of research and survey activities, including a great deal of traditional knowledge on the environment, its resources, and their management. Unfortunately, Commonwealth Science Council support for the Project ceased unexpectedly in May 1988. Since then, the Project has continued on the basis of the unremunerated services of the Project Organizer, the Research Organizer, and the Project Support Group. Among other things, this break has frustrated action to establish a proposed Marovo Education and Training Network — regarded as crucial to the success of the Project and vital for the distribution and application of the traditional environmental knowledge already documented.

## Selecting investigators

While searching for individuals with the qualifications and experience suitable to the Marovo Project, the Research Organizer is mindful of criteria important to the Marovo people. Such individuals do, of course, have professional research ambitions. However, investigators must recognize that their first responsibility is to the community of Marovo. This implies the organizing, conducting, and reporting of their investigations in ways consistent with the needs of the community as revealed by the Project's objectives. Although some conflict between the academic objectives of investigators and the basic requirements of the Project might have been expected, in no instance has this developed. Quite the contrary, for those investigators who previously had not been involved in such participatory research, the experience has proved stimulating and gratifying, bringing rewards considerably greater than that provided through academic results alone.

The Research Organizer makes recommendations to the Marovo Project Support Group regarding the suitability of potential visiting investigators. The Support Group assists the visiting investigator in the cumbersome and often frustrating task of obtaining the required immigration and research permits for entry to the Solomon Islands. The Project Organizer is then responsible for introducing the investigator to Marovo and its informants. Inevitably, as they become settled, individual investigators establish their own networks of informants and guides, easing the responsibilities of the Project Organizer who, nevertheless, remains in close touch with all investigators.

## Training

Because of the emphasis on participatory exchanges of information, there has been no formal training in matters such as interviewing techniques. Training has all been conducted "on the job" and shaped according to individual requirements. Every visiting investigator accepts an obligation to impart some knowledge and skills to the Marovo people; and, in the participatory spirit, the investigators themselves often benefit from on-the-job training by their local counterparts. Now that a good general appreciation has been gained of the nature and content of Marovo traditional environmental knowledge, it is expected that more structured training will be provided for Marovo people intending to conduct their own investigations. This will build upon training already given in the documentation of oral history funded through the Canadian High Commission in Australia and conducted by the Cultural Affairs Office of the Western Province Government.

Some activities for recording traditional knowledge have developed spontaneously through Project partnerships. A number of Marovo residents who have worked as counterparts to visiting investigators have started their own follow-up research. Oral tradition, environmental knowledge, and resource management principles are now increasingly being recorded by these "counterpart researchers," working in their local language and employing documentation skills obtained through the Project's on-the-job training. This work is vital to the environmental dictionaries that are being prepared. Furthermore, several of the older master fishers and other environmental experts who contributed most strongly to the Project's investigation of marine tradition have since continued to write down their specialist knowledge in detail, being encouraged by younger people.

## *Marovo Environmental Knowledge*

Environmental knowledge is starting to fade in Marovo, particularly among younger residents who spend long periods at school away from Marovo and away from subsistence activities. It is still widely possessed, however, by those who remain actively involved in traditional subsistence activities at sea and on the land, including many people of the younger generations.

The Marovo people's knowledge and understanding of their environment is a complex system that has evolved over a very long period. Although termed "traditional knowledge," "traditional" does not imply "static." What makes a local knowledge system "traditional" is its firm roots in the past, with a specific origin in indigenous culture and the local environment. Such continuity is a basic feature of any traditional system. The capacity of such systems to adapt, borrow, and innovate means that change is also a vital characteristic. Tradition is often unwritten, based not only on what each generation learns from the elders but also on what that generation is able to add to the elders' knowledge.

Local knowledge of fish and other marine animals, and their ecological contexts, is primarily behaviour oriented, focusing on information required to find and capture. This knowledge is based on first-hand observation of fish in the fishing ground and has been accumulating through generations, each new generation verifying aspects of the previous generation's knowledge through its own experiences. When talking about a certain item of marine knowledge, active Marovo fishermen will often say, "My father told me about this, but I had to see it for myself before I could really trust it. So I went out to the reefs and found out about it, and now I know."

Through these processes, most "inherited" items of knowledge are retained. Also, aspects that become less relevant for fishing may fade and, as a response to new developments in the local fishery, new aspects are added.

Although an appreciation of the ecosystem concept may be lacking in Marovo environmental knowledge, ecological linkages are often well understood. Depletion of a resource, seen as growing scarcity or decreasing mean size of a species, is quickly perceived and noted. Although depletion is regarded by some people as inevitable (but certainly "not a good thing"), the idea of a "rest" period for stocks to build up is a part of traditional resource management practices, now as before. Some fishing methods are perceived as destructive to the marine environment and the resource base. This particularly applies to dynamite fishing, which is occasionally practiced by a small number of people. The problem with dynamiting, many experienced fishers say, is twofold. Not only does it kill all fish, both large and small, that are present at the moment of explosion, but the explosions also destroy the coral stone, which is the home of the fish; therefore, there will seldom be "good fishing" again in a reef area that has been "bombed."

Local ecological understanding also appreciates the possible negative consequences for the reef and lagoon environment of large-scale logging, mining, and commercial fishing. Much discussion now occurs in Marovo about soil erosion, river-carried sedimentation, lagoon currents and reef siltation, and ecological interactions in the lagoon between stocks of food fish and bait fish harvested for use elsewhere by commercial tuna fishing boats. These contemporary examples of complex, indigenous ecological models are all underpinned by generations of accumulated understanding of processes in the coastal and marine environment.

## Documenting Traditional Environmental Knowledge

The Marovo Project was initiated by the Marovo people. This logically influences the approaches chosen to document traditional knowledge. For one, it is important that all scientific work be closely integrated with "local ways" so as not to be perceived as something external to Marovo. A high degree of local influence over the research process is taken for granted by most Marovo people involved with the Project. This decisive approach on the local level has no doubt tended to frustrate some visiting investigators, particularly those whose stays have been short and whose research designs have been based on tight logistic schedules and predetermined priorities. However, such initial frustration has often evolved into a deep appreciation of a unique form of close partnership in research.

Marovo villagers show a preparedness to "take charge" of the visiting investigator, not just by providing food and housing according to customary hospitality but also by guiding the day-to-day work of the visitor, thereby influencing the research process itself. In many ways, Marovo society seems to be highly participatory in relation to visitors, drawing visiting investigators into daily practical life and village discourse. Facilitated by the widespread command among villagers of conversational English, this process nevertheless requires the willingness of the visitor to eat local food, to engage in conversations on a great variety of topics, and to listen, learn, and teach.

The following approach to documenting traditional marine knowledge emerged during 18 months of continuous work by the second author.

At Marovo, the emphasis was on following and respecting traditional channels of authority. This implied that, even after clearance by the Marovo Area Council, practical issues such as places of residence and entitlements to fish were settled by seeking customary permission from the chiefs and other leaders concerned, such as master fishers. Similarly, when seeking information the investigator consciously attempted to use the established networks of specialists, visiting and talking with those recognized as the Marovo experts (or "leading persons") in their respective fields of knowledge. This pattern of "parallel clearance" — by the Marovo Area Council at a general level and by chiefs and other leaders for the specific villages visited — has become the norm for new Project investigators and for guiding their documentation efforts. It is generally taken care of by the Project Organizer resident in Marovo, who is a well-respected local politician and traditional leader.

As much as possible, visiting investigators are encouraged to learn traditional skills and information by doing, rather than just listening. In line with both the "personal observation" approach to environmental knowledge and the "participatory" emphasis of the on-site research process, investigators often find themselves on the fishing ground, in the gardens, or in the rain forest together with their "informants," the informants becoming practical teachers, showing the visiting novice how to apply traditional knowledge. Such was the approach continuously taken in documenting some 60 different fishing methods. In Marovo, it is often emphatically stated that "only by doing it and seeing it yourself can you find out whether what they tell you is true," and project investigators are often told by elders in scholarly terms that after the "theoretical" come the "practical" lessons.

Marovo people greatly enjoy conversation, and experts on fishing knowledge are no exception. Typically, much documentation work takes the shape of information exchange rather than formal interviewing. As the visiting investigators are regarded as experts within their respective fields, their Marovo counterparts generally ask them questions. The second author once acted as interpreter during a lengthy discourse between an expert Marovo fisher and a marine biologist of high international standing on the subtleties of courtship and spawning among a group of small coral reef fish — seemingly insignificant, as they are not eaten locally. It transpired that the Marovo expert had observed a number of things unknown to Western science. In Marovo, such discursive research is firmly reciprocal in nature, to the point where an anthropologist tells a legend from his native country "in exchange" for a Marovo legend just narrated, and where a marine biologist is asked for advice on how to efficiently get rid of sharks after Marovo experts have explained the lunar spawning cycles of the barracuda. Such reciprocal discourse typically leads to further fruitful exchange of ideas, as when the prospective shark fishers react to the received wisdom of shark biology by adding their own knowledge of lunar periodicity in shark aggression.

When visiting villages for the first time, investigators are encouraged to give talks to the community at large, explaining their work and answering questions. These sessions, usually held in the church or village meeting hall after the evening meal, have often developed into lengthy exchanges of information in which most of the adult members of the community participate. During the more successful of such meetings, a give-and-take process develops, whereby newly documented information is presented to the community, becoming the basis for further discussion. Such prompt feedback of traditional environmental knowledge in documented form sustains and stimulates the interest of Marovo collaborators, elders, and others who have provided information, and makes others more strongly aware of the nature and extent of the accumulated environmental knowledge that is part of Marovo culture.

# The Interview Process

Five languages are spoken in the Marovo area. All of them are related, however, and most people understand the Marovo language itself, which acts as a common language throughout the area. The majority of villagers also understand and speak Solomon Islands Pidgin, a mainly English-derived Creole language. Many younger people also have a good working knowledge of English. As is common in the Melanesian region, the Marovo people are capable linguists, many of them being comfortable with all five local vernaculars in addition to Pidgin and English.

This diverse linguistic picture has some consequences for Project investigations. Counterparts to visiting investigators are fluent in several vernaculars, Pidgin, and usually English. Thus, they act also as interpreters during interview sessions. Only long-term residence in Marovo makes it possible for investigators to become independent of interpreters; even then, local linguistic assistance is normally required when discussing subtle details of traditional knowledge with elderly specialists. Such is the case with Marovo taxonomy. As with other folk taxonomies, Marovo taxonomy — the naming and classification of fish, plants, animals, topography, and other aspects of the environment — has a structure considerably different from that of Western science. Although there are many cases where a Marovo fish, plant, or animal corresponds with species of Western science, such correspondence is far from general.

Many visiting investigators have had previous experience in the Melanesian region, and have found their knowledge of Melanesian Pidgin (of which Solomon Islands Pidgin is but one of three forms) to be a great asset, not just during interviewing but particularly during informal interaction and participation in village life. Whatever the gender of the visiting investigator, knowledge of Pidgin is a prerequisite for free and active conversation with Marovo women, most of whom are reluctant to speak English.

As for the interview process, "informants" are not usually "chosen" by investigators; rather, they present themselves or are recommended by authoritative persons as and when appropriate. Marovo elders are the key to much traditional knowledge and generally the highest authorities on matters relating to the customary law of resource management. However, many younger active specialists in restricted fields — such as net-fishers, underwater spear-fishers, and dedicated gardeners — also have a recognized status as "keepers of knowledge." To teach the deeper detail of environmental knowledge as related to practical activity, elders often recommended such specialists to visiting investigators.

There are important gender differences in the distribution of environmental knowledge. For example, whereas men generally possess the widest and most detailed knowledge of the marine environment, women have unsurpassed knowledge of the near-shore zone and its fauna of shellfish and crustaceans. Marovo women have a particularly close awareness of the phases of the moon because of their relationship to menstruation cycles. As women usually gut the fish catches, and so are able to observe changes in gonad condition, they have developed an intimate knowledge of the relationship between lunar stage and the reproductive cycles of important food fishes. Whereas the uphill primary rain forest is generally the domain of men, the low-hill garden areas are largely the domain of women. Old women are the gardening counterparts of master fishers, and it is these women who possess the deep and detailed knowledge about cultivating innumerable varieties of staple crops. For example, the senior women of one Marovo village could immediately list more than 100 varieties of ngali nut (*Canarium* spp.).

The Marovo Project has a policy regarding payment level for Marovo individuals who are assigned to assist visiting investigators. Payment is set to cover the cost of being unable to do "regular" work, such as fishing or gardening. In the Project payment policy, there has been a conscious effort not to appear

to be rewarding an individual for contributing to what is funda-
mentally a community Project, a project of "whole Marovo."

The question of payment for information, however, has occasionally arisen. Most visiting investigators have, under guidance from
the resident Project Organizer and others, grasped key Marovo
concepts of general reciprocity and have avoided any direct
payment of money. Reciprocity by the visiting investigator is
directed toward

- Coworkers (including main "informants"), taking the form
  of gift-giving and perceived as arising from a friendly and
  mutually rewarding social relationship;

- Households with which investigators live, taking the form of
  day-to-day contributions of food and other store goods; and

- Villages in which an investigator spends time, taking the form
  of donations to church, school, etc.

In several cases, investigators have maintained contact and reciprocity with individuals, families, and villages after leaving the
Solomon Islands.

## Reporting, Outputs, and Consequences

Reporting on the progress and results of the Project is required
not only for technical agencies of the Solomon Islands Government but also to keep the Marovo community informed and
involved. In general, investigators are required to produce at least
an interim written report before they leave. Copies of all reports
are filed with the Research Organizer and supporting government
agencies. Reports are available in whole or in part to other
interested agencies of the Solomon Islands Government.

Usually, more is expected than only a written report. Many
investigators, for example, have given seminars on their work.
These seminars are held in Honiara — through, for example, the
Extension Centre of the Fiji-based University of the South Pacific

— and attended by government officers and others with interest in the subject, not the least of which are Marovo people resident in Honiara. Also, investigators are encouraged to report to local communities visited in the course of the investigation.

At each Marovo Community Workshop, verbal reports are given on Project activities undertaken during the previous year. Investigators present in Marovo at the time make their own presentations; other presentations are handled by the Project Organizer, Research Organizer, or a Marovo person who worked in close collaboration with a particular investigator.

When information gained by investigators is also used for academic purposes, copies of any published articles must be sent to specified number of Solomon Islands Government agencies, including the National Museum, National Library, and Western Provincial Government, as well as to regional institutions such as the University of the South Pacific and the University of Papua New Guinea. The Solomon Islands National Museum has also suggested that copies of research reports be deposited in the libraries of Marovo primary schools, in line with the national policy on promoting local feedback on research results.

Copyright restrictions may apply to some reports or parts of reports. With respect to the traditional knowledge documented by visiting investigators in Marovo, copyright remains with the Marovo community, held in trust by the Project. However, the founding Project document (March 1987) clearly states that permission for investigators to publish traditional knowledge that they have helped to record "will not be unreasonably withheld."

Direct and tangible outputs of the Marovo Project include a large number of interim and final reports on specific Project activities as well as more substantial reports for different audiences, such as those of Johannes and Hviding (1987) for the Marovo community, Hviding (1988a) for fisheries managers, Johannes (1988) for fisheries scientists, and Hviding (1988b) for social anthropologists. A set of "technical dictionaries" are being prepared, entries and glosses in each being presented in one of the four main Marovo area languages: Bareke, Hoava, Marovo, and Vangunu. These dictionaries will cover terrestrial and marine plants and animals, together with general environmental terminology and technical vocabularies. Each typically has upwards of 400 entries (see Vaguni 1988). A series of booklets of local "custom stories," some of which embrace elements of environmental knowledge, is also soon to be published (for example, Vaguni and Hviding n.d.; Hviding n.d.).

Some indirect consequences of the Marovo Project approach to documenting traditional environmental knowledge should also be mentioned. A selection of Project material has inspired some recent efforts in developing secondary school curricula in the Solomon Islands (such as the *Resources from the Sea* unit for Form 2, currently under trial in Solomon Islands schools ) and in the United Kingdom (Barrett et al. 1989).

Subject to future funding, a "complex" of three related workshops on the Marovo Project will be held. The three workshops will cater to the community, technical (government planning and management), and academic groups. They will overlap and interlink to enable each group to understand the perspective and contributions of the others. They will also be used to examine the Project's attempts at "participatory planning" and to consider its effectiveness in contributing to community-based conservation efforts. Further, the workshops will assess the relevance of the Marovo Project for other traditional land- and reef-holding communities in the Solomon Islands and elsewhere in the South Pacific. The reports and guidelines that will come out of this innovative workshop experience are expected to be of widespread interest.

# References

Barrett, P., Button, I., Burt, B., Baines, G. 1988. Only One Earth: a multi-media education pack. Part 5: Ocean fisheries. World Wildlife Fund, London, UK.

Hviding, E. 1988a. Marine tenure and resource development in Marovo Lagoon, Solomon Islands. South Pacific Forum Fisheries Agency, Honiara, Solomon Islands. FFA Reports Series.

_____1988b. Sharing paths and keeping sides: managing the sea in Marovo Lagoon, Solomon Islands. University of Bergen, Bergen, Norway. Thesis.

_____ed. n.d. Katiga vivinei tuari pa Ulusaghe. Stories and legends from Marovo, New Georgia, in four New Georgian languages with English translations. Cultural Affairs Office, Gizo, Solomon Islands. (In preparation)

Johannes, R.E. 1988. Spawning aggregation of the grouper, *Plectropomus areolatus* (Rüppel), in the Solomon Islands. *In* Proceedings of the 6th International Coral Reef Symposium, Townsville, Australia, 8–12 August 1988. Commonwealth Scientific and Industrial Research Organization, Canberra, Australia. Vol. 2, pp. 751–755.

Johannes, R.E., Hviding, E. 1987. Traditional knowledge of Marovo Lagoon fishermen concerning their marine resources, with notes on marine conservation. Commonwealth Science Council, London, UK. Technical report, 23 pp.

Vaguni, V. 1988. Dictionaries of the plant resources of Marovo, Solomon Islands. Paper presented at Nga Mahi Maori o Te Wao Nui A Tane — A workshop on ethnobotany, Rehua Marae, Christchurch, New Zealand, 22–26 February 1988.

Vaguni, V., Hviding, E., ed. n.d. Katiqa vivinei pa Vahole pa pinato Hoava. Stories and legends from Vahole, New Georgia, in Hoava language with English translations. Cultural Affairs Office, Gizo, Solomon Islands. (In preparation)

ि‌

# THE AFRICAN SAHEL

*The African Sahel is a belt of land 300 to 500 kilometres wide stretching from Mauritania on Africa's Atlantic coast to the Sudan and Ethiopia on the Red Sea. It is bordered to the north by the Sahara Desert and to the south by tropical Africa. SOS Sahel International, a network of European and African nongovernmental organizations (NGOs), works with the rural peoples of the Sahel by supporting community actions that focus on conserving natural resources and increasing family food production. The following two papers provide a desciption of the SOS Sahel Oral History Project. The first paper is an abbreviated version of the project's final report and describes how traditional knowledge about ecological change and past agricultural and conservation techniques can directly benefit a development project; in this case, the implementation of a community forestry program. The second paper presents a personal account of a community researcher who worked on the project.*

# Documenting Oral History in the African Sahel

Aid and development workers, or "experts" as they are often styled, have a propensity to assume they are close enough to the reality of rural living to make informed decisions on behalf of the local population. Although this is sometimes the case, development work has tended to impose ways of thinking and structured work programs that are neither suited to nor supported by those people they purport to help. The Sahel Oral History Project (SOHP) has attempted to challenge the received image of the passive, grateful beneficiary who has been taught to fish or to farm. SOHP has given some 500 men and women, all classic development "targets," the chance to talk back, to broadcast their experiences, priorities, and perspectives.

Striking a balance between traditional land-use practices, the policies of governments and aid donors, and current pressures on natural resources is of crucial importance to ensure the sustainability of Sahelian agriculture and pastoralism. SOHP aims to set the current situation in its historical and cultural context, calling upon the memories of those who have lived through a century of unparalleled environmental change.

In providing the opportunity and space for Sahelians to talk for themselves, SOHP has taken a step toward recognizing that it is

By Rhiannon Barker and Nigel Cross, SOS Sahel UK, London, UK.

the participants in development projects who are the leading actors. It is with them that a dialogue should, and must, be set in motion. It is their agenda that counts.

## Background to the Sahel Oral History Project

SOS Sahel UK is a British voluntary agency and member of SOS Sahel International, a federation of European and African non-governmental organizations (NGOs). It works with rural people across the Sahelian zone of sub-Saharan Africa supporting community actions and initiatives that focus on conserving natural resources and increasing family food production.

Through a community forestry program in the northern Sudan, it became clear that there was a tremendous amount of vivid, untapped knowledge about recent ecological conditions that could be of considerable benefit to program activities. Frequently, village elders would tell program staff about the ecological changes (usually for the worse) that had occurred during their lifetime. They would also describe past agricultural and conservation techniques. SOHP was initially conceived as a way of recording this knowledge before it disappeared and, at the same time, involving elderly people more constructively in development planning.

In most long-term environment projects, the elderly tend to play a very marginal role. They usually are too frail for hard, voluntary labour, are economically inactive, and rarely get the chance to discuss project objectives with the planners. They are simply too old to be perceived as major beneficiaries. Thus, although elders are respected and honoured by their communities, development projects often fail to profit from their knowledge and experience.

By talking at length with farmers, pastoralists, refugees, and other economic and social groups, SOHP hoped to advance an understanding of traditional land use, land tenure, farming, and pastoralist systems, as well as the causes of desertification and many other aspects of Sahelian life. The aim was not only to record indigenous knowledge and improve rapport with local populations but also to develop a practical methodology that could be incorporated into project planning, implementation, and evaluation.

Social change in the Sahel has been rapid. Many children now have access to formal education, contributing to a loss of cultural continuity. Young villagers and outsiders increasingly consider traditional knowledge to be out-of-date. Recording traditional knowledge not only can rescue it from oblivion but can also demonstrate its value to a younger generation. Environmental and economic pressures in the Sahel have combined to create a period of unprecedented social upheaval. Academic descriptions of economic changes and illustrations of changing land-use patterns derived from satellite imagery fail to capture the subjective aspects of theses upheavals and lack the authenticity of first-hand testimony.

## Project Area: the African Sahel

Interviews were conducted from June 1989 to July 1990 in eight Sahelian countries: Burkina Faso, Chad, Ethiopia, Mali, Mauritania, Niger, Senegal, and the Sudan (Fig. 1). In 1973, the Francophone West African states established a forum for collective action against drought. Their definition of the Sahel excluded the Horn of Africa, effectively dividing the Sahelian zone in two. By including Ethiopia and the Sudan, SOHP is adhering to the geographical definition of the Sahel adopted by the International Union for the Conservation of Nature and Natural Resources (IUCN), SOS Sahel, and others, which defines the Sahelian region as a contiguous zone of low rainfall (60–150 millimetres per year), poor soils, and sparse vegetation dominated by *Acacia* scrub.

Most interview sites (Fig. 1) were linked to ongoing development projects. Thus, participating agencies have been provided with new, village-authored extension and evaluation materials, and, at the same time, SOHP has benefited from logistical and staff support. Although it is never easy for projects to provide such support, in general there has been a high level of cooperation.

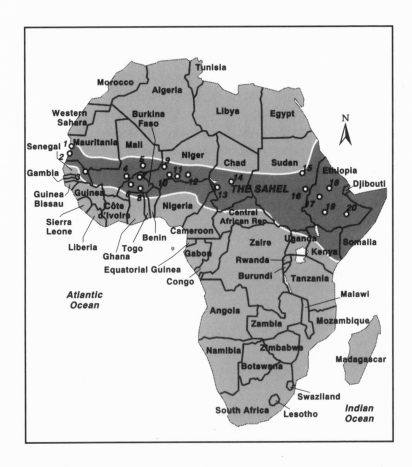

Fig. 1. Interviewing sites of the Sahel Oral History Project. Mauritania: 1, Nouamrhar; 2, Nouakchott. Senegal: 3, Bakel. Mali: 4, Gao; 5, Tominian. Burkina Faso: 6, Sapone; 7, Ouahigouya; 8, Gorom Gorom. Niger: 9, Takieta; 10, Tabalak; 11, Tabiri; 12, Zinder. Chad: 13, Mara; 14, Oum Hadjer. Sudan: 15, Shendi; 16, Wad el Hileau. Ethiopia: 17, Shewa; 18, Wollo; 19, Boubon; 20, Borena.

Interviews were also conducted in nonproject areas, but project sites tended to be easier to work in. Extension workers were familiar with both the area and the people; however, it was sometimes felt that their presence inhibited or biased certain lines of discussion. Between project and nonproject sites, perceptions of environmental and social change were very similar. The most frequently observed difference was the tendency of nonproject communities to regret the lack of a project. People on project sites tended to have a heightened awareness of environmental management and conservation techniques such as the planting of trees, shelterbelts, and soil improvement.

In selecting the project areas over the eight countries covered, a major consideration was the tribal, economic, and social groups that should be interviewed. Targeted groups included refugees (economic and political), pastoralists, farmers on rain-fed land, farmers on irrigated land, and fishing communities. At completion, interviews had been conducted at 20 different sites (Fig. 1) and in 17 different languages. A total of 450 interviews were completed, about half being with women. Most interviews were one-on-one, but some were with groups, bringing the total number of informants up to 650.

## *Project Guidelines and Questionnaire*

A guide for interviewers outlining a standard methodology and a flexible questionnaire were used as the basis for all interviewing work. Initial research for the guidelines took place in the UK in consultation with development agencies, academics, and available literature. A preliminary interview outline was written and tested in the Sudan. Further consultation and feedback from informants led to a number of changes. Discussions were also held with development workers on each interviewing site to establish their own priorities.

The questionnaire outline was flexible. To allow for the uniqueness of each interview and to acquire the necessary depth of information on specialized topics, the interviewer was encouraged to explore issues of particular importance or interest, while omitting other questions not relevant to the informant. Similarly, questions were added or subtracted depending on the specific country or site and according to the relevant political, social, and environmental conditions.

To draw up a questionnaire that can be used effectively in eight countries of different economic, social, and cultural groupings is a near impossible task. Questions that would strike a European as being neutral and rather mundane, such as "How many children do you have?," may prove offensive to some Sahelian mothers. To divulge such facts to a stranger may be tempting fate — some would say an open invitation to God to take a child away. Thus, sensitivity and consultation are necessary at all times.

Cultural bias in the interview outline is inevitable, although it can be reduced through thorough consultation. Moreover, the interviewers were given the scope to exclude anything they felt unsuitable and were encouraged to include questions of their own design.

# Selecting Interviewers

## Profession and Level of Education

Interviewers were selected from among journalists, extension workers, and students. The most successful interviewers were good communicators who had a natural curiosity and interest in the respondents. Although a high level of education and literacy was important to grasp the complexity of some of the questions and to aid the transcription process, levels of motivation and enthusiasm were also key factors in determining the success of the interviewer. In the fieldwork, transportation problems, inaccessibility of informants, and difficult living conditions inevitably led to frustration. Thus, the energy and enthusiasm of the interviewer was regarded as more important than previous interviewing experience.

Literacy was a prerequisite in this project. However, as interviewers were required to transcribe the tapes, future work by extension workers using oral history techniques will not necessarily require this ability.

Interviewers had to be fluent in the local language. Ideally, they were from the interview area; this promoted a more immediate rapport between the informant and the interviewer. However, such compatability was not always possible and, for reasons of education, most interviewers were recruited from the cities.

## *Gender*

To avoid marginalizing women, one male and one female interviewer were sought for each site. The Sahelian countries in which SOHP was working all have strong cultural and religious influences that tend to restrict the movement of women and inhibit easy communication between the sexes. For this reason, women interviewed women and men interviewed men.

Employing women proved much more difficult than employing men, largely because of cultural constraints restricting the freedom of women to travel. Having located female interviewers, the project coordinators found that they has less work experience than the men and generally needed more training and confidence building.

Despite the extra work involved, the policy of employing women was critical to the success of the project, particularly because men and women in Muslim societies live in separate social spheres. On some occasions, as an experiment, men were asked to interview women and women to interview men. Their comments on this experience were enlightening. The women, who might have complained that the men found their questions impertinent, generally found the interviews ran smoothly. The men, on the other hand, appeared at a loss to know what to ask the women and their interviews quickly broke down. Some men said that they found talking to women boring and unenlightening.

## Training Interviewers

In each country, the interviewing process lasted about 1 month. In this time, one or two sets of interviewers were recruited and trained, and interviews were conducted on up to four different sites. Such a tight schedule did not allow much time for training; however, a short program was devised that proved an invaluable component of the work.

### Day 1: Review

On the first day, interviewers are assembled and each question is discussed. Examples of previous interviews are shown and analyzed. If there is time, interviewers role-play by asking each other questions about their own lives and experiences. Role-playing can lead to a discussion on a wide variety of issues, including the pros and cons of various interviewing techniques. For instance, one person may play the "insensitive interviewer," looking away as the subject replies, yawning, and being inattentive. The subject is unaware of the interviewers instructions. After the exercise, the feelings aroused in the subject by such treatment are examined. Other roles include the "reluctant informant" and the "monosyllabic informant."

### Day 2: Interviewing

The trainer carries out the first couple of interviews, using the interviewer as an interpreter, thus giving a clear idea of the form that the interview should take. The "looseness" of the interview structure must be stressed, with the trainer showing how to follow up the interesting points with new questions. The process is slow and tedious, especially if the trainer does not speak the local language, but is effective in demonstrating tried and tested interviewing techniques.

## *Day 3: Write-up*

The interviewer writes up one of the interviews that they have conducted (in English or in French) to give the trainer a clear idea of the depth of information they have collected. Following this, the trainer points out areas where more information could have been sought, showing how to probe more deeply into relevant issues.

# *Selecting Informants*

Initially, SOHP intended to conduct interviews solely with elderly people, with their richer memory of social and environmental change. As the project progressed, however, younger people were also interviewed. This allowed comparisons to be made between the differing perceptions of the two generations. Thus, although the majority of interviews were conducted with the elderly, a few younger informants are also included in the sample. On each site, workers sought to interview an equal number of men and women.

As a rule, people with specialist knowledge were not sought; the project tried to canvass a fairly random cross section of the rural population. Before the interviews, those assisting in the project — usually the village chief, the head of the women's association, or an extension worker — were asked to identify the different social classes and economic groups in the community. This would ensure that the interviewers covered as wide a spectrum as possible. The majority of informants were farmers or pastoralists; but specialists such as the midwife, hunter, traditional healer, blacksmith, and village chief were also interviewed.

With a clear idea of the social, economic, and ethnic groups present in the interviewing area, the next step was to select and locate the sample to be interviewed. In most cases, candidates were contacted through traditional channels of authority, such as the village chief or the head of the women's committee. This was often time consuming; however, with the interviews endorsed by respected members of the community, informants had greater confidence and generally appeared more willing to cooperate. Local project staff were also useful in helping to establish links with the local community, although the elderly are likely to have more respect for their traditional leaders than for staff on development projects.

The selection method was not random: the sample, averaging perhaps 12 men and 12 women per community, was too small and the logistics were too complex to allow random selection. Some informants were selected by the chief, others were chosen by village groups, and some were too busy to talk or simply suspicious of the questions and unwilling to participate.

In situations where people lacked a well-established structure, such as refugee camps, selection was more haphazard. If a community leader could be identified, the channel of communication was relatively easy. Most often, however, refugee camps lacked ethnic and social homogeneity and therefore had no elected representatives. Project staff had to wander from house to house making their own introductions. Informants, however, seemed prepared to accept this intrusive approach.

# Interview Method

## Group Interviews

Most interviews were conducted with individuals, but there were also a small number of interviews with groups of up to 15 people. The project's main interest was specialized knowledge on the environment and work practices, as linked to personal histories and anecdotes from individuals. Group interviews were useful in providing consensus accounts. In a group situation, individuals are often animated by the discussion and follow through certain lines of enquiry in greater detail than they would in a one-on-one encounter.

## Location of Interviews

Most interviews were conducted in private homes or in the shade of a convenient tree. Sometimes, the village chief would call people to the village square or to the chief's house. Men, without domestic chores, were generally happy to be interviewed away from home. Women preferred to be interviewed in the house; not only was it socially unacceptable for them to be seen sitting chatting in a public place, but also it enabled them to continue looking after the children, guarding the stove, or completing craft work.

There are several problems associated with interviewing in the open: the heat of the sun rapidly wilts both the interviewer and respondent; strong winds interfere with the microphone, affecting the quality of the recording; and droves of curious, often disruptive onlookers are attracted to the site. It is advisable, but not always possible, to find a sheltered, quiet location to conduct the interview.

## Length of Interviews

Interviews lasted from 40 minutes to 2 hours, although initial introductions, rapport building, tea ceremonies, and other hospitalities often extended this time. For an intense dialogue, 2 hours was the maximum recommended time. The interviewer, in particular, has to be constantly alert during the interview, thinking of the next question to be asked, encouraging the informant to talk, and looking for interesting areas of knowledge and experience to examine in detail. If the respondent wishes to say more after a 2-hour meeting, then another meeting can be planned for a later date. As the "fatigue factor" is high, no more than three thorough interviews should be planned in any one day. Also, there should be an obligatory break after 5 days of interviewing. If the interviewer is required to do more work than this, he or she tends to grow bored and tired, emotions that soon discourage the informant.

## Gender

Interviewing women demanded a higher investment of both time and energy. Women were harder to pin down, as their domestic chores could rarely be postponed — there was always grain to grind, wood to collect, or a meal to prepare. The men were more inclined to come and talk, or perhaps they were simply less worried about the consequences of laying down the task at hand. Moreover, male respondents seemed to be naturally garrulous, benefiting from the experiences of a male culture that sets aside time and space for communal debate. They generally talked with greater ease for long periods of time without faltering; women usually needed more encouragement. When encouraged to speak, women tended to be less critical when reflecting on their life, attributing their hardship to fate, rather than external factors that influence their position. This made it more difficult for the interviewer to follow up further lines of questioning.

The same questionnaire was used to interview both men and women. The strong environmental slant of the original questionnaire tended to exclude and ignore women's knowledge, particularly women who played peripheral roles in agricultural and economic activities. Thus, questions concerning children, domestic activities, and social customs were added to the questionnaire to make more of women's experience and knowledge.

Problems sometimes arose when men tried to take over or disrupt interviews with women. For example, husbands would decide that they should act as mediators between their wives (or other female relatives) and the interviewer. The effect of the male presence on the quality of the work is open to debate. In some cases, it appeared that the woman was reassured by male encouragement; at other times, the consequences were disastrous, with the woman feeling unable to talk about certain issues and the man asserting that he knew the woman's mind better than she. When women are interviewed in the presence of men, the men often laugh at the questions and responses, whereas they take their own contributions more seriously. On balance, every attempt should be made to interview women alone, without interruption.

## *Interviewing Problems*

One old man in the Sudan told the interviewer proudly that he could go on talking until he had filled all the cassettes in the interviewer's bag. After 10 minutes he was finished, and the interviewer could not think of anything else to ask.

This illustrates one of the most difficult aspects of oral history: getting people to talk openly and in detail about issues perceived by both interviewer and informant as relevant. By attempting to illuminate certain issues, in this case environmental change, the informant may feel restricted in terms of addressing other issues that are of personal importance. Also, the question–answer format is inevitably rather contrived and can be off-putting, especially if the interviewer sees the set of questions as an inflexible agenda.

Other constraints include failing memories, contradictory responses, a pronounced tendency to romanticize the past and denigrate the present, and the willingness of many informants to "play the game" — saying what they think the interviewer wants to hear. This final factor is particularly problematic. Many rural populations have been made to feel that their traditional techniques in agriculture, medicine, and veterinary care are in some way backward and unscientific. Rural people are aware that the educated elites, who come on sporadic visits, tend to promote new technologies, encouraging a more scientific approach to all aspects of life. For this reason, many rural inhabitants are reluctant to divulge methods of animal treatment, land conservation, or herbal medicine — they believe that, by doing so, they may be labeled as ignorant or out of touch with the "modern" world.

For example, in a camp of sedentary pastoralists in eastern Chad, interviewers attempted to explore traditional veterinary practices. Initial enquiries met with blank faces, shoulder shrugs, and denials that any such system existed. Only after the interviewers began to talk in positive terms about traditional techniques they knew of from other areas, did the informants begin to share their own extensive knowledge.

Finally, there is a problem of trying to search for common ground across the different modes of cultural expression. The desire for quantification and specificity that preoccupies research in the North is not an easy notion to convey to a Sahelian farmer. Efforts to find out the number of cattle in a herd will often provoke raised eyebrows, derisive laughter, and evasive responses: "God is generous, I have enough animals to fertilize my fields!" or "We have to make do with whatever God gives us." Such responses are not surprising if the question is equated to asking a European "How much do you have in your bank account?" Similarly, the question "How many hours does it take you to grind your corn?" may be answered "I begin when I return from collecting the water, and finish when my husband returns from the field."

Responses that involved figures, dates, weights, and times were often spoken in French or English rather than the local language. For this reason, the accuracy of ages and dates is questionable, as is the project's ability to collect specific quantified information.

## Recording, Translating, and Transcribing

All interviews were recorded, and interviewers were encouraged to take notes to supplement the recordings. Many interviewers found taking notes to be difficult, complaining that it slowed down the dialogue, distracted them from the questions, and caused them to lose valuable eye contact with the informant. Despite this, the value of brief notes was stressed as a useful means of reflecting on and ratifying certain points, providing backup for a bad or faulty recording, and for recording nonverbal expressions and descriptions.

Following the interview, the interviewer transcribed the tapes, usually translating them into French or English; on one occasion, the tape was transcribed into the local language and translated by a second party. This process is tedious and time consuming — adequate time must be set aside if it is to be done accurately. Transcription problems include translating local names for plants and animals, as well as more complex ideas and concepts that the interviewers find difficult to explain, except by resorting to their own interpretation and jargon.

An extension worker from Mali poignantly described the type of problem that she faced transcribing interviews from Bobo into French. Bobo, she explained, is rich with subtly worded proverbs that can not be easily translated into French or English. She cited the following example: "If you want to stop the mouse, you must first get rid of the smell from the *soubala* spice."

Apparently, this proverb refers to the value of a good upbringing. In the past, children were well brought up and, therefore, could be relied upon to behave well. Today, children fail to receive proper instruction from their parents and, for this reason, can not be blamed for behaving badly, just as the mouse is not to blame for taking the *soubala* spice when it smells so enticing. Given the complexity of the proverb, the extension worker decided to opt for the "comprehensive" translation. She was more concerned with conveying the meaning of the sentence, than in translating the words themselves (for a full account, see the next paper, *An Experience in Oral History: One Researcher's Account*).

Distortions of this type are inevitable. A more thorough examination of the level of distortion would be useful as a means of monitoring the extent to which the content changes from the point of verbal narrative to the written, fully edited interview.

## Constraints

Analysis of the material collected has revealed that the project has not recovered as much indigenous knowledge, in its specifics, as was originally thought possible. For instance, recipes for medicines, meals, and organic fertilizers, and accurate descriptions of plant uses, changing vegetation, animal numbers, and herd composition are often mentioned only in vague terms.

It is interesting to speculate on the reasons for this inability to collect fuller and more specific details of traditional practices and indigenous knowledge. Some obvious constraints have already been identified, such as the respondents' possible fear of appearing ignorant if they divulge knowledge of herbal remedies or local traditional veterinary practices to a "more scientifically educated" audience. Moreover, there is the problem of finding some system to express numbers, sizes, dates, ages, and weights that can be understood by both cultures. Also, there are some practices that must remain secret, for to give away the secrets of the village is a dangerous betrayal. On one site in Mali, for instance, nobody admitted to any knowledge of botanical methods of abortion, although extension workers knew that they existed.

It is difficult to know how such constraints can be effectively overcome; however, in terms of project methodology, there are many questions that might be considered. Were interviewers asking the right questions? Would the project have benefited from having coordinators or interviewers who were more highly qualified in the field of environmental studies? Were field trips too short and interviews too brief? Or, do we all simply harbour too romantic a notion of indigenous knowledge? Traditional knowledge, after all, is not static — it evolves to suit a changing environment. It must be open to the acceptance of new equipment and technologies. Farmers and pastoralists will adapt to use whatever method serves them best, be it traditional or modern, old or new; there is no nostalgic attachment to archaic practices.

In an attempt to answer some of these questions, SOS Sahel is now considering a pilot study in the Sudan that will involve some comparisons between local memory, colonial officer memory, and extant documentation.

# Results and Conclusions

## Analysis of Results

The findings of such a broad, multifaceted study as SOHP are hard to quantify. However, what can be usefully highlighted are common themes, which occurred from Ethiopia in the east to Mauritania in the west, and either challenged or supported the current orthodoxy.

The common experience of environmental and climatic change and the reason attributed to such change was universal: "The bush is dead, the trees have disappeared, and the soils are tired." The reason cited by almost every informant is inadequate and sporadic rainfall. Human factors were also cited: pressure on land from rising populations and the fact that more and more pastoralists, whose herds have been devastated by drought, are turning from pastoralism to farming. Bush land is being cleared with increasing rapidity to make land available for cultivation. The increased pressure on land and natural resources has disrupted what was a previously amicable relationship between farmers and pastoralists — conflicts between the two groups are frequently reported.

Although the majority felt that degradation was attributable to climatic change, many were confident that steps can, and are, being taken to counter some of the damage. Trees are being planted and the fertility of the soil has been improved by adaptations of traditional farming methods such as compost holes and binds to reduce soil erosion and improve water infiltration. Development projects have clearly been instrumental in adapting and reinstating many of these traditional techniques. Such work is freely commented on by the informants, who forcefully state their own agenda.

Traditional knowledge concerning the environment and systems of farming and pastoralism have been touched upon. Farmers talk about tried and tested methods of improving soil fertility. Pastoralists explain how they control animal reproduction, the pastures preferred by each of their animals, and the ideal ratio of males and females. Healing methods used by traditional mid-wives and herbal remedies gathered by the Marabouts (traditional healers) are mentioned in varying degrees of detail.

Despite the constraints and the lack of detail in some areas, SOHP has succeeded in establishing a fuller picture of community history and social evolution than originally anticipated. It has revealed unexpected changes in relationships between groups: adults and children; sedentary farmers, pastoralists, and agropastoralists; men and women. Much of the information contradicts received development wisdom and provides ample evidence that many standard generalizations simply do not stand up or are so general as to be seriously misleading. For instance, the project highlights the dangers of generalizing about women's position in rural communities. According to Fatchima Beine, President of the Women's Committee of Tabalak, Niger,

> Before, when natural resources were abundant, women did not have to work so hard. Now, however, women do the same work as the men and, during the day, they work in the field.

But, according to Sayanna Hatha, a woman in the neighbouring village of Tabiri,

> New technologies have helped to lighten a woman's load. She no longer has to spend several hours a day grinding grain because of the presence of diesel-powered mills; there are wells and pumps from which she can collect water. The men plough the fields and if the family doesn't have enough food, then it is the men who have to go in search of supplements.

As always, there are marked differences within villages that are lost in generalizations. As reported by Rekia, a woman farmer in Takieta, Niger,

> Years ago, all the wood we needed was near. It used to take us only 5 minutes to collect. Now it's a 10-hour trip. So, those who can afford it, buy it from the men who sell it in the market.

As far as fuelwood collection is concerned, the gap between women with some money and women without has widened.

In the Nile province of the Sudan, married women whose husbands have remained in the area as farmers welcome their improved quality of life. This is illustrated in the words of Um Gazaz El Anada from Misektab (near Shendi),

> Now we don't have to pound the *dura* or pull water from the deep well. Also, our participation in agricultural work has decreased.

and Hajey Juma Ahmed,

> When I was young, I used to do some work on my husband's farm. But now women are just sitting at home waiting for the men to bring money to them.

But the widow of a pastoralist in the same area has had to work as a paid seasonal labourer and is the sole breadwinner for a family of eight.

Such variation in women's roles and status within a well-defined geographical area illustrates the perils of generalization. Many interviews with women highlighted the phenomenon of female heads of households. As a follow-up to these findings, a research project has been planned that will look closely at this group's problems and potentials. The research will not only fill a gap in knowledge but also find a practical application on SOS Sahel projects.

## Application of Results

### Book publication

A book on SOHP is planned. It will present lightly edited versions of about 20% of the interviews to capture the authenticity and immediacy of the process and will provide a short analytical introduction drawing on all of the project material and highlighting the main themes and issues that arise. There will be a full cross-referenced index and black and white portraits of many of the subjects.

### Transcripts and index

A complete index of all the interviews will be available to researchers, development workers, and other interested parties. The index, which is currently evolving, will provide easy access to comments made on topical, political, social, and economic issues. It will eventually be published in an inexpensive form and made widely available at a modest cost.

### Development education

Living in the age of mass media, the Northern public has more information about the lives of Africans than ever before. But images of Africa are usually inextricably linked with "bad news": drought, famine, civil wars, and brutal dictatorships. This image tends to be unintentionally reinforced by the emphasis that fund-raisers put on starvation and drought.

SOHP has attempted to redress this imbalance by providing a long-term picture of people's lives. It cannot edit out the tragedies of disasters, as these are graphically described by those who have lived through them, but the same witnesses also demonstrate their ingenuity and tenacity, and reflect on the "good life." The interviews create a positive image of everyday Sahelian life: harmony with, and care of, the environment; the position of men and women on the land and in the household; and changes in family relationships and social customs. Individuals are no longer presented as emaciated victims or happy, simple peasants; instead, they talk directly about themselves. Their published words should be of value to aid agencies and other groups from the North working on development education who are trying to convey the realities of the African Sahel.

Initial feedback from the development education departments of a number of NGOs suggests that the interviews will add colour and life to the materials that they produce. The interviews are already proving valuable as a primary resource for writers on the Sahel. Interviews have been used in the Minority Rights Group Report on the Sahel, in a study in Burkina Faso commissioned by Oxfam, and by the editor of *Green Wars*, a Panos Institute report. Journalists traveling to the Sahel have used the interviews for background information. Such usage will increase on publication.

### Botanical and agricultural surveys

Scientific summaries of botanical and agricultural data are being collated for each project site by Dr Gerald Wickens, an economic botanist with considerable Sahelian experience.

### Guidelines for extension workers

Guidelines in interviewing techniques based on practical experience will be published for use by project extension workers.

## Application of the Methodology

Development projects are often caught up in an almost obsessive drive to produce quantifiable results that can be presented to donors as irrevocable proof of the project's success. Preoccupied in this search for measurable achievements, other more subjective parameters are either forgotten or ignored. In creating a dialogue between development workers and local communities, SOHP has demonstrated the value of improved communication at all levels of project activity.

Feedback from project sites where interviewing work has been conducted by extension workers has many spin-offs: it is an effective method for creating links with new communities and is a valuable training tool. The coordinator of the interviewing work in Mali noted in her report that the work provided her with a new training field, from which both she and extension workers have benefited. The work, she feels, is particularly important on new project sites during the community assessment, when all can "benefit from the stimulus of a rigorous questionnaire." She goes on to say,

> The general utility of this research to the project is that it does something to counteract the idea that farmers are ignorant, conservative, and fatalistic. Such preconceptions persist amongst our staff, although they are more subliminal than explicit. One of their effects is that little attempt is made to link the techniques we are trying to popularize with the farmers own experiments. Thus, the extension worker appears as a giver of solutions and the farmers own capacities are undervalued. And seeing themselves as surpassed, they are less likely to volunteer suggestions, further aggravating the imbalance.... The more details we have of farmers' knowledge and ingenuity, the more we can hope to counteract these problems of attitudes.

In the same vein, a Senegalese NGO (Fédération des paysans organisés du département de Bakel), that participated in the project noted the following:

> We wanted to participate in this project from the start because we realized that it would be of benefit to our own work.... We felt that it would be particularly useful to our literacy trainers. In this respect, the results have gone beyond our expectations. What might have seemed like a lot of extra work from the outside in fact worked to our advantage. We put out trust in young inexperienced workers and were delighted to discover that they were able to carry out the work well.... In addition, they discovered a rich well of knowledge. We have decided that we can not leave it here; we will continue the oral history work on the project.

Thus, not the least of the benefits of the Sahel Oral History Project has been its impact on the interviewers, nearly all of whom have acquired valuable new insight, often into their own communities. If oral history techniques are institutionalized in project work, they can have a very positive impact on the extension worker's depth of understanding and sensitivity toward the participating community.

It appears that the most immediate and practical benefit of the project has been in identifying the value to projects and project workers of taking the time to learn, through interviews, as much as possible from individual life histories and reflections. When such work is collected together, important "under-researched" areas become apparent and can be explored to ensure that the objectives of "developers" account for the many subtle variations in attitude and priorities of the individuals who make up the community.

# An Experience in Oral History: One Researcher's Account

---

*The following text is a direct English translation of an oral presentation given in French by Brigitte Kone. From Mali, Mrs Kone served as a community researcher for the SOS Sahel Oral History Project. To retain the flavour of the presentation, this account has received only a very light edit.*

Today, I would like to talk to you first about the area where the project was conducted, as well as the methods that were used. Next, I will talk about the problems I encountered during my research. Finally, I will mention the positive results of my study.

Our project, an oral history project, included seven villages. These villages form part of another large project on community development, for which I am the Women's Activity Coordinator. However, the seven villages in which I conducted my research are not the same villages as those involved in the community development project. My point is that I did a lot of traveling between the seven villages to carry out my research.

The vegetation in these villages is very similar to that of the Sahel, with hardly any trees. There is a lot of sand, many ravines, and the ground is flat. This is basically what the villages, where I conducted my research, are like.

I would now like to talk about my research methods. The questionnaire was completely new for me as it contained scientific terms. However, the project head helped me by explaining their meaning. This made the questionnaire much easier for me.

Before beginning my research, I visited the chief of each village, because where I come from, you can't work in a village unless the chief agrees to let you do so. The chief also chose the old men and women I was to work with. This was very valuable to my research. I also worked with storytellers and blacksmiths, men belonging to a particular caste. In fact, the questionnaire had to be translated from French into Bobo, the local language. This was pretty difficult, as I had to retain the meaning of the questions.

The problem I had when conducting this study was the mistrust of the villagers. Their mistrust of people, because of ethnic group, is by nature very great. This is because we all have secrets and we don't want to pass these secrets on to anyone who is not from the same village. This is why people always mistrust one another.

You have to know people for a long time in my ethnic group to gain their trust. Once you have gained the trust of my people, you can be comfortable working with them and be sure you have their trust. To achieve this, we have a tradition: to gain someone's trust, you give this person gifts, especially if he is an older person.

Therefore, when I went to interview the old people, I took along either kola nuts, tobacco, or I bought them a *dolo*, the local beer. This made them very happy. Each time I went to see the old people, I brought them a small gift and they would be happy to speak with me.

Another act of diplomacy I made use of, is that often, when I went to see the old person, who may have been sitting under a tree among the rubbish, I would sit down beside him or her to show that I was on the same level. And when I would buy them a *dolo*, which I don't normally drink, the old people would make me drink it to test me, to see if I could take it. So I'd take the *dolo* and I'd drink it. Also, there were meals that weren't all that healthy. I'd accept the meal and I'd eat it, just to gain their trust. This helped to make the people appreciate me, which made my work much easier.

Another problem I had, the worst problem, was transcribing things. It's very difficult to translate ideas from Bobo into French, because you have to translate without changing the idea. And the people speak in images. They never speak directly, they always make allusions to something. I, therefore, had to translate everything correctly, to do justice to the original words.

For example, an old woman told me that if you want to get rid of a mouse, you have to get rid of the smell of *soubala*. *Soubala* is a spice you put in sauce to increase its flavour. It has a strong smell, and the mice in the house will look for it and take it. So if the mice looks for that because they could smell it, you have to get rid of the smell of soubala to get rid of the mice.

I had problems with this image, which was new to me. It was hard for me to understand this idea and translate it into proper French. This shows that the amount of knowledge passed on to the children by the old women was incredible. According to the old women, the children were well educated in the past. Now they are not well educated, and she said that this wasn't the children's fault, but the fault of the mothers in this generation, because they are not properly educating their children. That's what the proverb was all about: rather than getting rid of the mouse, you should get rid of the smell of *soubala*. This means that rather than accusing the children, because they are poorly educated, accuse the mothers.

Another problem I encountered was the dictation machines. There were two of us carrying out the study: myself and a man. And there was only one machine. Whenever he needed the machine, I was using it. We got in each other's way. This made it pretty difficult for us.

Now I want to tell you about the positive effects of the study. The research allowed me to trace my roots, to discover where I really came from. This is because I discovered a lot of things in the very area I worked in.

Because my family is Christian, I had never had the chance to see a fetish. But this time I saw one. I was shown one. I saw what a fetish is. A fetish can be a stone, it can be a very simple stone, it can just be a pot, and it can be an animal's tail. And the traditional Bobo believes in his fetish. Because they're farmers, they won't work the earth without consulting their fetish. They won't do anything without consulting their fetish. The fetish represents God for the traditional Bobo. Sacrifices are often made to the fetishes. The animals used for sacrifices are goats or sheep, and chickens are often used, or a type of food like gruel is offered to the fetish.

I even had the chance to see a creek, the village chiefs took me to the creek to show me the sacred spot. In the past, there was a spring that bubbled up out of the ground at this place. This was something extraordinary for them. There were always fish in that creek. There's a fetish in the creek beside the spring, and every year they make offerings to the creek. I had the chance to see this.

I also discovered something about the local trees. We have several different kinds of trees. I discovered that each tree is used for a traditional medicine. We trust traditional medicine much more than modern medicine. I also discovered that the local trees are often used by artisans. For farming, there's the pickaxe; all farming tools are made using the trees.

Something else I discovered, another interesting detail: the location of the hearth in a house. I did not know that in the past, the kitchen hearth had a special spot. I found out that the hearth is always facing the west of the village the house is in. I asked why. They told me that the dead are buried so that the husband faces east and the wife faces west. The wind, which comes from the west, carries the smoke with it. This way, the smoke won't get in a person's eyes.

We really believe in this because for us, the dead are not really dead. They are still alive and their lives and their spirits have to be preserved.

The other positive point for this project was the accessibility of the villages. We can now reach all seven villages easily. The large community development project also benefited. And this year, it was very easy to choose the new villages, because we have already established a certain amount of trust.

I would also like to emphasize the education of the farmers. The farmers also learned a lot through their oral history, because the project made the farmers aware of their own problems. They have become more aware of the situation they are living in.

From my position, I was lucky, because when they tell the name of certain trees, it's hard for me to describe this tree. So my role was to find out the trees' scientific names. These names are in my translation. I wrote down the local names of the trees, and then I had the chance to do some research on my own, to discover the scientific names of these trees. This was a step forward for me, too.

That's about all I have to tell you. I am very happy, because the research gave me the chance to find my roots.

ॐ

# NORTHERN THAILAND

*The Mountain People's Culture and Development Educational Programme (MPCDE) was founded in 1980. Since then, it has been concerned with documenting and applying the traditional environmental knowledge of the mountain cultures in the "Golden Triangle" of northern Thailand. The following two papers, by MPCDE staff Leo Alting von Gesau, Sanit Wongprasert, and Prasert Trakansupakon, present some of this work. The first summarizes preliminary results of an IDRC-sponsored project on regional development. Traditional environmental knowledge is examined in light of how it has adapted to social change and to what extent it has been incorporated into development ventures. The second paper specifically describes MPCDE's efforts to document and apply the traditional environmental knowledge of the highlanders of northern Thailand. MCPDE's work is meant to create an awareness of existing development problems and their possible solutions among program staff, interviewers, informants, and villagers by focusing on tradtional ecological, managerial, historical, and ritual knowledge.*

# Regional Development in Northern Thailand: Its Impact on Highlanders

For centuries, the northern region of Thailand has served as a refuge for minority peoples of neighbouring countries. Only 1% of Thailand's population consists of mountain minority tribal peoples. Some, such as the Karen and Lawa, have lived there for centuries. Others, such as the Akha, Hmong, Htin, Khamu, Lahu, Lisu, and Yao/Mien, have migrated to the region because of various political, economic, and other social pressures in their native lands. Such migrations began in the middle of the 19th century and continue today.

There are now between 530 and 600 thousand tribal minority peoples living in some 2 200 villages and other locations dispersed throughout the remote highland areas of northern Thailand. These highland communities pose political, administrative, economic, and social problems for the Thai government. However, they also make an important contribution to the region's economy.

Highland languages are quite distinct from Thai, as are their customs and laws. Highlanders have become known for their

By Leo Alting von Geusau, Sanit Wongprasert, and Prasert Trakansupakon, Mountain Peoples' Culture and Development Programme, Chiang Mai, Thailand.

sophisticated cultures, key to which is their intricate adaptation to, and knowledge of, the ecological environment.

## Economic Issues

The Thai government and some scholars have argued that the excessive production of annual crops on steep slopes through swidden (shifting) cultivation has damaging effects on the forests and watersheds. However, some authorities suggest that swiddening is ecologically, economically, and socially appropriate given the requirements of small communities in tropical or subtropical environments. Monocrop systems are viewed by some as the only viable alternative to swidden agriculture. However, some recent studies have shown damaging effects of these systems on the mountain ecology of northern Thailand.

In 1967, it appeared that more than 2.24 million hectares of forest had been seriously affected by shifting agriculture in northern Thailand, and that this figure was increasing by 40 thousand hectares every year. Some scholars, however, have disputed these findings and criticized the conclusions drawn from remote sensing techniques. Whatever the case, the state of northern Thailand's forests is serious, and may ultimately lead to economic and social disturbances in the country. Agricultural, reforestation, and social forestry programs have been initiated to cope with this situation (in, for example, the Sixth National Program of Thailand: 1986–1991).

## Social Issues

The Opium Act of 1959 banned the sale and smoking of opium in Thailand. As a result, both opium growers and smokers faced a drastic change in lifestyle, something that the Thai government had to deal with.

The opium poppy grows best in a cool climate and at altitudes above 1 000 metres. As such, it has been an ideal cash crop for the impoverished mountain populations of Thailand. Also, it should be noted that opium addiction is not a cause of impoverishment; rather, it is a consequence of health problems and impoverishment.

In 1965, the United Nations Survey Team on Economic and Social Needs of the Opium-Producing Areas in Thailand set out to determine the extent of opium production. The Team used two methods in its survey: interviewing and aerial survey with ground inspection. By the 1980s, the Thai government was able to reduce opium production through effective law enforcement, crop replacement, and education. An especially large drop in opium production was observed between 1984 and 1986.

At the same time, however, several government agencies and functionaries have also questioned the regional development impact of these programs on both opium-growing and non-opium-growing highland communities; the latter accounting for about 80% of the highland population.

## Political Issues

Before 1983, many political problems arose from the infiltration of highland tribal communities by insurgent elements. These problems no longer exist (*Bangkok Post*, October 1986); however, the highland people are still seen as a minority group whose language, economics, sociocultural customs, and religion differ from those of Thai lowlanders. Highlanders are therefore often seen as having no sense of national belonging or national consciousness. They are seen as separate, cohesive groups.

Illiteracy, poor health conditions, low life expectancy, and insecure socioeconomic conditions are common problems in the highlands. These problems are being aggravated by a slow influx of highlanders from neighbouring countries, the result of political oppression in Myanmar and the changes occurring in Laos after the Vietnam War. As well, the poor lowland peasantry of Thailand and ethnic Chinese from Yunnan Province, People's Republic of China, have been migrating to the Thai highlands.

As a result, incorporation policies formulated in 1967, such as the formal granting of Thai citizenship, are behind in their implementation. In some provincial districts, the proportion of the population with Thai citizenship is as low as 10% (National Statistical Office 1986). The land rights of highlanders is another problem that remains unresolved.

To tackle these issues, the Thai government, with the help of various international agencies, has implemented the highlanders' development program. The objectives of the program are to

➤ Stabilize the residence and secure the livelihood of highland peoples;

➤ Discourage and eventually replace opium production;

➤ Discourage and stop deforestation; and

➤ Encourage highlanders to participate as citizens in the national life of Thailand.

Since 1969, at least 22 government agencies and many international donors have been operating in the highlands of Thailand. Today, the international agencies supporting projects of education, health, and crop replacement include the Australian Development Assistance Bureau (ADAB), the Food and Agricultural Organization of the United Nations (FAO), Canada's International Development Research Centre (IDRC), the United Nations Development Programme (UNDP), the United States Agency for International Development (USAID), the United States Department of Agriculture (USDA), and the World Bank (Tapp 1985).

These and other agencies, the projects they have supported, and the six national development programs introduced after 1961 (the last one being 1986–1991) have increasingly emphasized regional development. Within the region, they have focused on social issues, local involvement, infrastructural arrangements, and action research.

Beginning in the 1960s and continuing today, many programs were implemented to develop the Thai highlands. However, only since the 1980s have studies looked at the impact and implications of development programs on highland communities, including Lee (1981), Cooper (1984), and Tapp (1985, 1986). Although valuable, these and similar works have several common flaws:

- All deal with only one tribe, specifically the Hmong and some minor sections of the Akha;

- Several deal in a limited scope with one or a few villages and thus are micro-oriented;

- None are comprehensive, focusing on only one or two issues, such as opium or cash crops;

- None deal with the regional perspective as intended in the regional programs;

- Most do not deal specifically with the impact and implications of regional development;

- None address policy-making; and

- Several are doctoral theses, intended more for academics than for policymakers.

## *Environmental Knowledge*

Since early 1987 and the discussions on swidden agriculture, deforestation, reforestation (with eucalyptus and pine trees), and land use in general have escalated in the northern highlands of Thailand. Debate has focused on the question of blame. Who is at fault for the escalating deforestation, depletion of land resources, erosion, and illegal logging: the mountain peoples themselves or, rather, government or commercial agencies? In the last few years, this debate has culminated in discussions on land rights, land use, and the resettlement of hill tribes in the Thai lowlands.

At the same time, some development agencies, government organizations, and nongovernment organizations (NGOs) have begun to focus on the "social" or "cultural" dimensions of development. In some cases, issues of "indigenous knowledge," "indigenous management," and "traditional medicine" have been included in projects descriptions. However, little has been done to determine which social and cultural elements and which indigenous environmental knowledge could become integral elements of development.

Thus, in analyzing the impact of regional development upon highlanders in northern Thailand, the following questions must be answered:

- What has been the impact of massive resource depletion and environmental degradation on the traditional environmental knowledge of the hill tribe population?

- To what extent has modernization and consumerism, through increased road access or new educational systems, eroded the traditional environmental knowledge of the highlanders?

- How well have mountain populations adapted to environmental degradation, resource depletion, loss of land, etc., through adjusting and employing their traditional environmental knowledge?

- To what extent have development projects seriously accounted for "indigenous knowledge," "traditional technology," "indigenous management," and "traditional environmental knowledge"? This would include traditional herbal medicine and medical treatments, the use of ethnobotany in agriculture (knowledge of soils, water, fauna, flora, and natural pesticides and fertilizers), knowledge about nutrition, handicrafts (materials and colouring), indigenous education (oral texts and songs), and laws and value systems related to the environment.

The participation of tribal peoples and the use of their resources is key to successful regional development. Recently, however, it has been recognized that many existing development programs suffer some serious deficiencies (see Chayan Vaddhanaputhi 1986), including

➤ A lack of information on the highlanders, their communities, and their responses to regional development efforts;

➤ A lack of foundation on policies that were based on past research in the social or natural sciences;

➤ A lack of involvement by tribal people in both development and research;

➤ A lack of trained personnel to carry out the work; and

➤ A lack of commitment by Thai officials for long-term research.

A recent document from the Thai Ministry of Education (1987) goes so far as to say

> The government should analyze and research all dimensions of activities directed at hill-tribes and employ these results in the revision of government policies and operational programmes of all Ministries and Departments concerned [and] provide an information-base on peoples and conditioning in the hills [as a means for this revision].... If the current trends in the northern mountains and government action...are not soon corrected, a definite negative impact on the lives and cultures of these people, the environment, and national security will ensue.

## The Project

In December 1989, the Mountain People's Culture and Development Educational Programme (MPCDE) began a 2-year comprehensive, comparative, and interdisciplinary study to look at
the implications and impact of regional development programs
on the highland communities in the Chiang Rai region. The
project is sponsored by IDRC and is part of the Southeast Asian
research network involving "tribal people" in Malaysia, the
Phillipines, and Thailand, centred in Kuala Lumpur, Malaysia.

The project was conceived to improve our understanding of the
various highland communities and their responses to regional
development programs. Specifically, the objectives of the proposed study are as follows:

- To collect and document basic demographic, socioeconomic,
  and ecological information on regional development programs and government policies in the highlands of northern
  Thailand;

- To examine and analyze the social, political, economic, and
  ecological implications of these regional development programs and their relationship to migration, settlement
  schemes, land rights, citizenship, reforestation, and forest-
  protection schemes;

- To evaluate how quickly ecological changes affect the traditional environmental knowledge of the mountain peoples;

- To examine the extent to which highlanders adapt to ecological change through the use of traditional environmental
  knowledge;

- To determine the roles of the various agencies that are responsible for policy, planning, and implementation of regional
  development programs in the highlands of northern Thailand;

🌿 To study the impact of regional development on highland communities and to document, at the grass-roots level, the responses and reactions of highlanders to such programs;

🌿 To examine the extent to which development programs have accounted for social and cultural values such as indigenous management, indigenous laws and norms, traditional educational values, traditional knowledge of flora and fauna, and indigenous skills related to the ecology;

🌿 To systematically evaluate regional development programs and government policies while recognizing the views of the highlander peoples;

🌿 To define the problems and needs of highland communities in relation to regional development programs and to publicize this information to policymakers and planners;

🌿 To examine the problems related to reproduction and conservation of flora, fauna, and related knowledge and skills, and to determine to what extent the highland peoples see them as economic assets for their future; and

🌿 To provide feedback and recommendations to improve current and future regional development programs in the highlands of northern Thailand.

## Project Area

The northern highland region of Thailand (Fig. 1) encompasses 40% of the country's territory, covers 2 of the country's 17 provinces, and is home to almost 6 million of Thailand's 60 million people. Mountainous areas make up 65% of the highland region and 35% of the country. In the past, the highlands have been characterized as "wasteland"; more recently, they have been seen as a "resource area."

Chiang Rai Province is located in the northernmost part of Thailand. With an area of 11 678 square kilometres, Chiang Rai shares its border with Laos in the east, Phayao in the south,

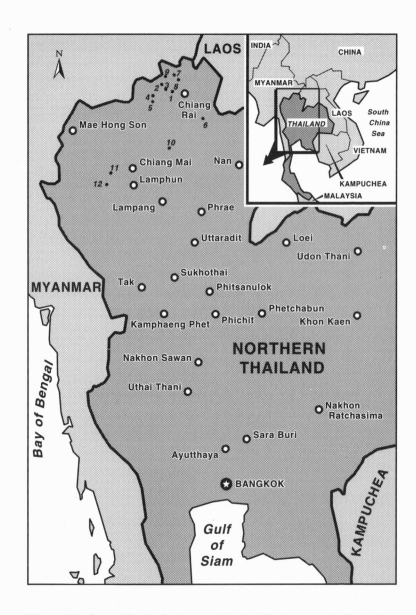

Fig. 1. *Northern Thailand: home of the highland peoples. The twelve villages visited were in Chiang Rai and Chiang Mai provinces: 1, Doi Lan (Lisu); 2, Doi Chang (Lisu); 3, Doi Chang (Akha); 4, Thung Phrao (Karen); 5, Thung Phrao (Lahu); 6, Mae Ta Maew (Akha); 7, Ayo Mai (Akha); 8, Pha Dua (Yao); 9, Huay Mae Liam (Yao); 10, Mae Poon Lang (Lahu); 11, Khun Tae (Karen); 12, Mae Chorn (Meo).*

Chiang Mai in the southwest, and Myanmar in the north and west. The southern border of Yunnan Province, People's Republic of China, is about 200 kilometres from the northern border of Chiang Rai. The prominent geographical features of Chiang Rai are mountains and, until recently, forests. However, over the last 20 years, the forests of Chiang Rai have been rapidly disappearing.

In 1988, Chiang Rai was divided into 11 districts (Amphoe), 103 subdistricts, 1 093 villages, and 539 hill tribe villages. The main ethnic groups are the Lahu, Akha, Hmong, Lisu, Karen, Khame, Yao, and Lawa. There are also large numbers of Yunnan Chinese, Shan, Lua, and Wa. The largest population of highland ethnic minorities is in Mas Chan District (41 080 persons), followed by Mae Suai District (20 611 persons) (National Statistics Office 1986). The study will concentrate on these districts and their hill tribe villages.

## Administrative Structure

The project employs three "professional" staff: a project administrator (Director, MPCDE), a research trainer and coordinator (Assistant Director, MPCDE), and a field coordinator/researcher (Senior Staff, MPCDE). The main functions of the professional staff are

➤ To initiate and implement the research project;

➤ To train field staff in research methods, including the design of questionnaires;

➤ To train interviewers and assist in field trips;

➤ To coordinate and manage research projects with other MPCDE programs, mostly consisting of students and collaborators from different mountain areas and highland villages; and

➤ To tabulate, analyze, and report project results with the help of other technical MPCDE staff.

There are two groups of field researchers: the MPCDE-related research team and the village-based helpers or coresearchers.

The MPCDE team consists of about 14 researchers-in-training. All are part of the Chiang Rai/IMPECT All Mountain Peoples' Program, either as staff or as students (that is, they are all affiliated to an MPCDE program). Almost all team members belong to a highland tribal group; there are four Akha, two Yao/Mien, three Lisu, two Hmong, one Karen, and two "non-tribal" members that speak Akha. Education levels range from sixth grade high school to college or university.

The village-based group consists of 24 helpers or "coresearchers." As 12 villages were to be covered in the study, this represents two people per village. Group members might be village heads, teachers, or other literate persons of the village. Education levels vary from sixth grade high school to teachers college.

## Selecting Researchers

The most important attributes for community researchers are curiosity, analytical capacity, and an understanding of their own culture and how to conduct research among their own people. Motivation is also key. Most of the village-based researchers as well as the MPCDE team receive only minimal remuneration for their work.

Community researchers must also have the confidence and respect of the villagers. They must have a thorough knowledge of the languages and cultures of the region, as well as a good understanding of the effects of "development" on villagers. They must be fluent in their own tribal language and be able to immediately transcribe from their own language into Thai (mountain languages have no script). They must have the ability to get "inside" information.

Community researchers must possess a good traditional, tribal education and awareness of their own culture. Also, an education level of at least sixth grade high school in the Thai educational system, which is high for the mountain peoples, is required. They must also be able to work as part of a team and cannot be closely associated with any "big" development project.

As interviews always involved people of the same gender, it was essential that the village-based team have a strong representation of both men and women.

## Training Researchers

Training for this vast research project was mostly conducted in the field. It began in an informal setting with the MPCDE research team obtaining an overview of the main development problems as perceived by the villagers. Having gained the confidence of the villagers, the research team introduced more sophisticated survey methods to obtain more in-depth information. Through the surveys, the community researchers discovered that many of the problems of their own villages were common among other tribal groups.

As the research progressed, other methods were introduced, including interviewing and participant observation. Issues and problems were reviewed from the bottom up. Discussions looked at problems through the eyes of the villagers, and followed a brainstorming approach.

Next, the basic socioeconomic, demographic, ecological, political, and structural data and problems were covered. A base-line approach was used in an informal a setting as possible. This enabled the project team to grasp the "setting" of the problems in the 12 villages. This was followed by household surveys: individual interviewers (researchers) providing a detailed overview of the villages.

## Selecting Informants

Village "informants" were usually elders with a thorough knowledge of the history of the village and a detailed understanding of traditional knowledge. The same persons would also be subjects for the household interviews. Other informants included village heads and school teachers, both having a good understanding of the village from the "inside." Informants were selected by the MPCDE research team and some field research staff.

## Interview Methods

Interviews were conducted in 12 villages throughout Chiang Rai Province and part of Chiang Mai Province, northern Thailand (see Fig. 1). Several interview methods were used: from brain-storming sessions to more structured team interviews with senior villagers (base line) to household-based interviews.

Household interviews were conducted by local interviewers with the help of an MPCDE team member. They proved to be the most difficult stage of the project, resulting in the resignation of a few local researchers. Less formal, more group-oriented interviews worked best. In such a setting, villagers did not feel as if they were being "interrogated," as was the case in individual interviews.

The highlanders of northern Thailand have a strong sense of freedom and autonomy within a Thai context. Because of this and the flood of researchers, anthropologists, developers, and missionaries who have come to question or "develop" them over the last 30 years, the highlanders tend to be skeptical and shy in front of interviewers. Like any other people, they dislike answering questions about their personal or economic affairs unless they believe that, by doing so, their life will genuinely improve or they will be recognized for who they are and what they have to offer.

Consequently, interviews were held inside the villages, where the tribal researcher met and spoke with friends, relatives, and acquaintances in an informal setting where people would feel comfortable sharing their knowledge with the "outside" world. Also, the words "interview," "interviewer," and "questionnaire" were avoided. These are words of the social scientist, equating people with objects of academic research.

The first team and group interviews were informal and spontaneous. Household surveys tried to be equally spontaneous, but, by necessity, ended up being somewhat more organized and formal. They took place either in peoples houses or in village fields.

The length of the interview depended on the interviewer and the informant. A compassionate and interested interviewer might stay overnight with an informant to gain as much information as possible. Team interviews lasted anywhere from 2 or 3 hours to an entire day. Interviews of a single persons by one or two interviewers and household overviews averaged 1 or 2 hours. In many cases, interviews were conducted a little at a time. Except for team interviews, researchers always interviewed persons of the same gender.

## Translation and Recording

There are as many as 12 mutually incomprehensible languages among the mountain peoples of northern Thailand. As such, "inside" information is best obtained through one's own language; "outside" information is obtained through a common language, which is now increasingly Thai, but sometimes Lahu or Chinese.

Interviews are done in the village's own language and by native speakers. However, questionnaires are in Thai, which all team and staff members can read. The MPCDE research team is responsible for designing and translating the questionnaires. This is done during periods of rain or when villagers are busy in the fields (planting, weeding, or harvesting).

Most interviews were recorded in writing, translated, and transcribed. If an informant was uncomfortable with such a procedure, researchers memorized the information. The information is then compiled in tables designed by the MPCDE research team, analyzed, and interpreted. Occasionally, cameras, video recorders, and tape recorders were used.

## Managing and Interpreting Data

Team base-line, household base, and other related information is compiled in village dossiers. The information is then tabulated by the MPCDE research staff. They also perform the first review, analysis, and interpretation of results. When the first phase of the village overviews is finished, the analysis and conclusions are discussed with MPCDE-related research team and reviewed with the field staff.

## Preliminary Results

Preliminary results clearly indicate some common problems in the villages of northern Thailand.

### Land rights

Villagers have no legal rights regarding ownership or even usufruct of land. In fact, one village had been told by the Thai Ministry of the Interior, which deals with problems of national security, that it would have to vacate its site; a site that the village has occupied for more than 30 years. At the same time, the Ministry failed to indicate where the villagers might resettle.

In the Mae Chaim, Mae Suai, and Mae Chan areas, it appears that large lowland companies are able to rent or purchase land near or even within village fields. Company activities include coffee production, agrobusiness, and forestry. As land in the mountains cannot be legally bought or sold, villagers find this situation very puzzling, and the results can be quite disturbing.

For example, land used to plant rice or cash crops is lost, resulting in increased malnutrition and disease. Also, companies employ villagers at very low wages; some companies pay their workers only once every 3 or 4 months. As a result, employees borrow money from the companies to buy food, money that is repaid through wage deduction, leaving some people without income.

Some companies also run gambling operations, in which villagers loose their money.

## Suicide

The project team has also noticed the appearance and dramatic rise of a phenomenon hitherto unknown among the highlanders: suicide. Usually accomplished by drinking of strong insecticide, about half of the suicides occurred among younger, unmarried people, mostly girls. The main reason for this trend appears to be the growing disparities in wealth. A small number of families are becoming richer and a majority of families are becoming poorer. This is creating marriage problems in the villages. Among the Lisu, for example, the poorer boy may no longer be able to pay the bride-price for the girl he wishes to marry. In despair, the girl takes her own life. In the case of the Karen, several young couples have committed suicide because their parents would not permit their marriage. Other suicides are the result of young villagers being unable to seek a new future in the cities and feeling "trapped" in the mountains.

## Drug abuse

A similar phenomenon is the dramatic increase in drug abuse. Alcohol, opium, ganja, and heroin addiction is on the rise in most highland villages. Over the last 2 years, the number of addicts has doubled or even tripled in some villages. Villagers attribute this trend to deteriorating health conditions and an increased sense of "futurelessness." Another cause is the deterioration of family relations, particularly between men and women. The role of the highland man has corroded more quickly than that of the woman. This leaves a heavy burden on the woman, resulting in marital friction and sometimes divorce. Younger girls often make their way to the city in search of a husband or a brighter future; however, this often leads to prostitution and drug abuse (see Chivit Bondoi 1990).

## Citizenship

In 10 of the 12 villages studied, villagers complained about their inability to obtain household registration or identification cards giving them Thai citizenship. Despite years of effort by village leaders to obtain citizenship for their people, it appears that such documents have recently become even more difficult to obtain.

## Water supply

Most villages do not have an adequate water supply. There seems to be two reasons for this: increased deforestation for commercial purposes and, according to the villagers, increased temperatures over the last few years leaving streams dry during periods of no rain.

## Road access

During the rainy season, roads in and out of highland villages are impassable. These roads were originally built for reasons of national security or to allow easy access to forests by the Royal Forestry Department. As the threat of communism has subsided and much of the forest has been denuded, there no longer seems to be an interest in maintaining the mountain roads. Only a few of the larger, Chinese market towns near the border have good road access and electricity. Tribal villagers believe that their economic interests are being neglected in favour of the city-based "national" economy.

## Preliminary Conclusions

From these and other preliminary observations, the following conclusions can be drawn:

- There is a tendency in village families to shift from subsistence farming to wage labour.

- Increasingly, children are being sent to lowland schools far from their native village.

- Among younger villagers, there is massive urban migration; however, migrants invariably lack the proper skills for urban life and end up working for very low wages.

- National or private family-planning projects, to some extent forced upon villagers, can create social and psychological problems, sometimes resulting in suicide.

- Increased contact with the "outside" and lowland world has resulted in an increase in new diseases.

- The generation and culture gap between the young and the old is increasing; the youth are not interested in the ritual ceremonies or traditional knowledge of the elders.

- Consumerism, entering by road, radio, and television, is creating unrealistic expectations about an artificial world of luxury.

- In many villages, tourism is encouraging and promoting opium smoking; inducing young children to beg; and, in several cases, devastating village fields and trees with elephant rides for tourists.

- Traditional medicines are still used, but mainly by the old and the rich, who have time to collect the medicinal herbs.

- As a reaction to massive deforestation and with the hope of gaining land rights, highlanders are beginning to plant fruit trees in the fields and to increase forest management around several villages.

- In areas of severe land loss, there is a tendency toward increased handicraft production and husbandry, especially cattle breeding.

## Final Products

The final product of the project will be a research report prepared by the research team. It will contain a combination of quantitative and qualitative results and conclusions presented in a comparative and contextual framework with an historical perspective. This type of report is essential for any study looking at development impact. Rather than being purely technical and quantitative, the report will give examples of how particular villages or groups react to negative impacts of regional development based upon traditional knowledge.

The MPCDE research is not intended for "outside" publication. Its principal purpose is to create an awareness of existing development problems and their possible solutions among participating team members, interviewers, informants, and villagers. In this context, the team will attempt to make the data relevant to forestry, wildlife and agricultural management, land-use planning, medicine, education, and cultural development.

## *References*

Chayan Vaddhanaputhi. 1986. Thai–German Highland Development Programme: social sector evaluation report. Thai–German Highland Development Programme, Bangkok, Thailand.

Chivit Bondoi. 1990. Life on the mountain. MPCDE, Chiang Mai, Thailand. MPCDE Newsletter No. 3.

Cooper, R. 1984. Resource scarcity and the Hmong response: patterns of settlement and economy in transition. Singapore University Press, National University of Singapore, Singapore.

Lee, G.Y. 1981. The effects of development measures on the socioeconomy of the White Hmong. University of Sidney, Sidney, Australia. PhD thesis.

National Statistical Office. 1986. Survey of hill tribe population. National Statistical Office, Office of the Prime Minister, Bangkok, Thailand. Survey No. 2529.

Tapp, N.C.T. 1985. Categories of change and continuity among the White Hmong of northern Thailand. University of London, London, UK. PhD thesis.

—— 1986. The Hmong of Thailand: opium people of the Golden Triangle. Third World Publications, London, UK.

Thai Ministry of Education. 1987. Conclusions of the Task Force appointed by Ministry of Education Order No. 609/2528. Ministry of Education, Bangkok, Thailand.

# Documenting and Applying Traditional Environmental Knowledge in Northern Thailand

Since its creation in 1980, the Mountain People's Culture and Development Educational Programme (MPCDE) has been concerned with the documentation and application of the traditional environmental knowledge of the mountain cultures in the "Golden Triangle" region of northern Thailand.

## The Akha Association, Chiang Rai

Within MPCDE, the strongest concern for documenting and applying traditional environmental knowledge has come from the Akha people. The Akha are a tribal group of mountain peoples numbering more than 1 million. They are spread over southern Yunnan Province (People's Republic of China), eastern Myanmar (Shan states), Laos, northern Vietnam, and northern Thailand. In Thailand, there are between 35 and 40 thousand Akha spread among 250 villages. The Akha language is part of the Tibeto-Burmese language family. Until recently, the Akha language did not have a script; however, over the last century there have been

By Leo Alting von Geusau, Sanit Wongprasert, and Prasert Trakansupakon, Mountain People's Culture and Development Educational Programme, Chiang Mai, Thailand.

attempts initially by missionaries and later by anthropologists to help develop a script.

The Akha word for customary law is *zang*. It includes all of the rules, regulations, customs, and laws passed down from one generation to the next to ensure the cultural survival of the Akha people. *Zang* also includes traditional knowledge about the rich local flora and fauna and how to use human resources to their full potential, living as a marginalized people in a difficult political situation. Much of *zang* is contained in the many oral texts of the Akha pertaining to different rituals and is often expressed in song. It also includes the practical knowledge passed from father to son, from mother to daughter, and from the elders to the younger generation.

Traditional specialists of Akha customary law have been the *Phi-ma* or *Boe-maw*, the teacher/reciter; the *Dzoe-ma*, or traditional village leader; the *Ba-djhi*, or village technician; and the *Nji-pa*, or shaman. For the women, there is the *ja-jeh-ama*, or the "older lady with the white skirt," who is generally in charge of agriculture in the fields. In most villages, there are also several herbal and handicraft specialists (both men and women). In general, elders, because of their experience, are considered to have more knowledge. In Akha society, the tendency is "to learn from others" and to "find out for yourself." Thus, in most villages there are many self-taught people (*na-nga*) in several fields.

The MPCDE/AFECT-Akha Association in Chiang Rai is aware of the strong ability and will of the Akha to survive as a distinct culture in times of great adversity. It is also aware of the desire of the Akha to integrate into Thai society as equals. The Association's awareness and concern for the preservation and integration of Akha culture stem from two observations: the loss of Akha traditional cultural values and the success of other minority peoples to preserve their traditional culture.

The Akha's loss of traditional values is due to many factors. It is due to the growth of Christianity, in particular the conversion of persons to more sectarian and fundamentalist groups. It is due to a loss of traditional skills, a loss of morality, and a loss of traditional social structure and sense of belonging. In contrast, the Chinese of Laos, Myanmar, and Thailand and the Hmong of northern Thailand are minority peoples that have managed to preserve their traditional culture. In both cases, as with the Akha, the question of "ancestor service" was a symbol both for those who wanted to preserve traditional knowledge as well as for those who wanted to abandon it.

Extracting and applying lessons from these observations is not easy. The idea of culture or of *zang* customary law is very complex. It is not clearly divided into the distinct fields of Western knowledge. Thus, penal law, civil law, morality, etiquette, and pure wisdom are not always clearly divided. This is also true for medical knowledge, agricultural knowledge, and managerial knowledge. In addition, the young tend to identify old culture with ritual, ceremony, or folklore and to reject it as old-fashioned.

Akha youngsters studying in Thai schools and living in a Thai environment (mostly away from their villages) are often unaware of the relative poverty of their formal education and the richness of knowledge present in their tribal culture. Because of discrimination, they may be reluctant to learn about and practice their own culture and thus may appear to be more Thai than Akha.

The Western opposition between old-fashioned and modern, backward and progressive, may also have become part of their thinking. Unfortunately, "modern" or even "Christian" in an Akha context might come to mean "easy"; "traditional" then becomes "difficult." In fact, Akha customary law has shaped remarkable people with remarkable knowledge. Christianity and modernity are producing, in our context, uninteresting or even weak people without the depth of traditional knowledge or even with a contempt for tradition.

Most Akha believe that "old" knowledge or customary law is not good because it is old or even because it is Akha. As for environmental knowledge, when the forests, plants, and animals begin to disappear, young Akha have no idea what the elders or songs are talking about. Similarly, the herbal specialist might be unable to find important plants, roots, and bark.

Several older Akha like to visit to the Chiang Mai Zoo. There, they can still see the animals of the old songs: tiger, bear, panther, and eagle, as well as anteaters, peacocks, deer, and many types of birds, monkeys, and snakes. Most of these animals have disappeared from the village areas in the mountains; for the young, these animals are strictly zoo animals.

In the case of plant life, there will never be a botanical garden to house the thousands of plants, trees, and herbs of the mountain areas that are now threatened with extinction. The number of indigenous species has been dwindling at an escalating rate, a rate that nobody could have foreseen in 1980, when MPCDE was founded.

## Teaching Traditional Knowledge

When teaching, documenting, and applying Akha traditional knowledge, a sharp distinction cannot always be made between ecological, managerial, structural, historical, and ritual knowledge. They are interwoven into all aspects of cultural life and expressed through song and spoken word.

Most of the work in documenting and applying the traditional knowledge of the Akha was carried out by the AFECT-Akha Educational and Cultural Centre in Chiang Mai. In 1990, this Centre had 40 students from several different Akha villages.

Founded in 1981, the Centre arranges for specialists in traditional knowledge to visit Chiang Rai. While in town, they teach Akha zang to the Akha students attending Thai schools. This has been going on since 1985, when the Centre was run exclusively by Akha managers and an Akha Committee. At the end of each school semester, students take exams in Akha *zang* as well as the regular Thai exams.

In addition to this program, efforts are being made to cover Akha culture more systematically in village schools. There are now Akha Association teachers in 12 Akha villages. The Thai government allows 20% of the teaching time to be devoted to Akha culture and traditional knowledge. However, teachers have insufficient training and receive little guidance about what should be taught.

## Traditional Medicine

From 1986 to 1988, the Chiang Mai Centre studied the traditional Akha knowledge of herbal medicine. Following this study, students were requested to look for medicinal plants in their villages and bring them to the Akha Association in Chiang Rai. A nursery was set up in Chiang Rai, but several of the plants could not survive the difference in altitude between the mountains and the city. As a result, some smaller nurseries were established at a few MPCDE mountain stations.

Ailing students and villagers were encouraged, even in Chiang Rai, to seek traditional medical treatment before seeing a "modern" doctor. In some villages, traditional healers received training in modern health care. Between January and August 1989, a collection of Akha herbal medicine was established and classified, and the Akha uses were translated. Following this, the Chiang Mai and Chiang Rai groups worked together to set up a system of primary health care for the villages that combined traditional and modern medical techniques. The team consists of a Thai doctor and a few young Akha from the Chiang Rai Akha Association who had received paramedic training and were working in the mountains.

A lack of funds means that these efforts are progressing slowly. However, the final intention remains: to develop a small, practical medical handbook combining traditional Akha and modern techniques.

## Breeding Chickens and Pigs

In the last few years, many Akha have abandoned Akha *zang* and turned to Christianity, purely because they could no longer afford the *zang* rituals, such as ancestor service. This was due to a shortage of pigs and chickens, which also resulted in increased levels of poverty, a lower population of fowl, and a general neglect of agricultural resources.

In traditional Akha law, *zang* rituals — including ancestor service, other field ceremonies, and sickness rituals (including funerals) — divide the protein supply among the villagers. The loss of these rituals and, hence, the loss of customary law destroys this sophisticated distribution system and threatens the nutritional well-being of the villagers. To help alleviate this situation, a cooperative chicken- and pig-breeding project has begun. This project is being coordinated through the Akha Association in Chiang Rai.

## Handicrafts

Another project in its early stages is the Association's handicraft project. Its purpose is to cooperatively design and produce handicrafts using materials unique to the region's ecology. The project is currently underway in 12 of the 50 villages that are covered by the Akha Association in Chiang Rai. The elders of these villages are recognized as knowledgable with respect to natural dyeing, the making of cotton, and the use of a diversity of materials from the forests and fields near the villages, such as rattan, bamboo, and certain types of reeds, flowers, insects, and seeds. The project is also consulting those villagers that are most skilled in the creation of intricate embroidery and the construction of baskets.

Like the project on traditional medicine, an important part of this project is gathering and classifying material from the flora and fauna. The work on handicrafts has aroused more interest in the Akha people than any other project, particularly among women. In the current situation of disappearing land and forest resources, handicrafts are becoming an increasingly important alternative source of income.

## Other Uses of Traditional Knowledge

Besides traditional medicine, animal husbandry, and handicrafts, the traditional environmental knowledge of the Akha covers several other "disciplines":

- Agricultural knowledge includes an understanding of soils, natural fertilizers, and traditional cash crop and forest products.

- The knowledge of water resources includes an awareness of underground currents, the location of water sources in areas of scarcity, and the hydraulic principles of water systems.

- The Akha knowledge of forest management is substantial. Even in heavily deforested areas, the Akha and other mountain peoples commonly maintain a forest belt around the village. This forest belt serves both economic and ecological interests. It is a source of medicine, food for both people and animals, and protection for some animals; it is also used to plant cash crops, such as mushrooms.

- Nutritional knowledge is reflected in the strict dietary rules of Akha customary law. Small village and field vegetable gardens often contain over 50 species of edible plants and herbs.

## Legal and Moral Issues

In addition to the wealth of traditional environmental knowledge present in Akha customary law, the Chiang Rai centre has addressed the legal and moral aspects of traditional Akha culture and customary law. When compared with modern Western systems, the traditional moral laws and regulations of the Akha are very strict. An effort has been made to retain these values in the Akha Association in Chiang Rai, including some of the dietary and nutritional rules of Akha customary law.

The Akha Association has been structured according to the rules of Akha egalitarian society. It has a bottom-up structure, as in the traditional Akha village. This contrasts the Thai social structure, which is mostly vertical. As well, the older people in the centre still serve as a "Council of Elders" and tasks are assigned as they would be in the mountain villages.

## Recording Traditional Knowledge

Since its founding in 1981, the students of the Akha Association in Chiang Rai have been documenting and cataloguing important Akha texts and customs. Texts are first recorded on tape and then transcribed and translated.

Three phonetic systems are used to record Akha oral texts. The first uses Thai characters, the second system is a more academic phonetic script, and the third uses Roman characters, of which several varieties exist. This third system was generally introduced by missionaries, and several Akha groups in Thailand and Myanmar have tried to unify the script.

Much of the traditional knowledge of the Akha is contained in song. With the passing of the older generation, however, many of these traditional songs are rapidly disappearing. As a result, the Akha Association has a large collection of audio tapes that capture this wisdom.

The Association also possesses a large collection of slides documenting the traditional agricultural cycle and traditional agricultural rituals. Photographic records also exist of handicraft techniques, cotton processing, dyeing and embroidery, forest management, and important rituals, such as the death ritual.

Recently, some of these events have also been captured on videotape.

# The Chiang Mai Centre

MPCDE/IMPECT-Chiang Mai is the main centre for research, documentation, and training regarding the cultures of Thailand's mountain people and the problems of regional development. Half of its staff consists of "traditional" tribal people, most with a professional or vocational education. Other staff tend to be from the other minority peoples of Thailand. Some of the part-time research staff are from IMPEC, the All Mountain Peoples' Scholarship Fund. Most are studying in high school; teachers, medical, or agricultural college; or university. These students share a great common interest in the traditional knowledge of their cultures. The Chiang Mai programs thus have a bond with many of the mountain villages, including those of the Hmong, Karien, Lahu, Lisu, and Yao/Mien in addition to the 60 Akha villages in Chiang Rai Province.

## Training

Training has concentrated on providing students and staff with a better understanding of their own background and villages. During their vacations, students and staff are expected to do action research in their own villages.

In 1985 and 1986, training was devoted to culture, law, and morality. In 1987, training concentrated on traditional education. In 1988 and 1989, training focused on traditional medicine and methods to document medicinal plants. In 1990, training focused on some very practical questions: How can the mountain peoples achieve self-determination and self-management? How does one operate photography and video equipment? How can traditional knowledge be documented? A great deal of time was also devoted to research training.

## Conserving Traditional Knowledge

Incited by the example of the Akha Association in Chiang Rai, other tribal groups have started to show an interest in documenting the traditional knowledge of oral texts and songs. They have also expressed an interest in setting up a project and association similar to the Chiang Rai model.

For example, a group of Sgaw-Karien in the Mae Chaem area of Chiang Mai Province have begun to organize a project, but funds have yet to be obtained. This group, some of them Christians, has also begun to realize that as the tribal elders die, great treasures of knowledge about life and the ecology may be lost forever.

Another stalled initiative is a project investigating how small, traditional, home industries of the highland communities could be adapted to the modern market. A small pilot project focused on village-based handicraft industries, including embroidery, silversmithing, weaving, and basket making — activities that are all based on traditional skills but also use "intermediate technology."

# APPENDIX

*This appendix presents the notes of the workshop rappor-teur, Dr Evelyn Pinkerton. Two additional presentations — one from the Amazon Basin and one from the Pacific Northwest of the United States — are summarized. The discussions that followed each presentation are presented here in a condensed form, and some of the issues that workshop participants identified as essential, common elements of research into traditional environmental knowledge are identified.*

# A Summary of
# Workshop Discussions

---

## Primary Presentations

### The DCI Pilot Project

As hosts for the workshop, the Dene Cultural Institute (DCI) was able to involve a wide array of project participants in its presentation and in the exceptionally lively discussions that followed. This direct illustration of the nature of Dene participation set the tone for the entire workshop. It provided a living example of the possibilities of research on traditional environmental knowledge (TEK).

Some Dene elders, who served as informants for the project, took part in the presentation. They spoke through an interpreter about their experiences growing up on the land: the harshness of climate, the strict instruction they received as young people about surviving on the land and dealing properly with all the natural resources in their territory, and the enduring respect and love they held for the land that supported them. The elders spoke from the heart in sharing their experience of the past and their hopes and fears for the future.

Dene interviewers talked about their experiences interviewing Dene elders alongside technical non-Dene researchers. A Dene cultural leader, author, and interpreter of Dene traditions to the outside world also participated in the discussion. All the Dene participants were able to situate TEK research within the broader political context affecting the Dene homeland.

One part of the discussion centred around Dene hopes that the research could assist them in a return to living off the land and in rejuvenating their entire culture, which had grown out of their experience with the land. The discussion touched on practical aspects of these aspirations. There were two sides to this discussion. Some Dene felt that resources were plentiful (at least for the number of Dene currently using them). Others felt that if everyone returned to dependence on the land, scarce resources would soon be exhausted. These same participants were dubious about the willingness of many Dene to abandon patterns of consumerism developed in recent decades. Both sides of this discussion were in agreement, however, about the political importance of documenting TEK. It was seen as a key step to understanding and fully demonstrating the current and potential impact of oil and gas developments on traditional subsistence pursuits. The Dene felt it would be impossible to make sound decisions about their future without the firm grounding in their traditions that TEK could provide. Thus, documenting TEK was seen to have direct implications for how aboriginal title, land claims, and comanagement agreements would be worked out.

The discussion also focused on the potential role of TEK in the school system. All the Dene participants viewed the educational system as often irrelevant and alienating to Dene children; it teaches them about farm animals and ways of using the land that they do not experience in their own environment. At the same tine, being in school removes Dene children from opportunities to learn about their own environment through participating with elders in winter subsistence activities such as trapping. They were being taught to be consumers of goods produced elsewhere, not learning how to produce for themselves. The Dene wanted the research to document traditional knowledge so that it could be taught to children in school. Without active intervention of this sort in the current educational process, they envisaged a lost generation that would have neither the ability nor the will to survive on the land, and no more than a limited ability to adapt to other modes of living.

The workshop participants had the privilege of directly experiencing the efforts of a group of young Dene to revive traditional drumming and singing. This group of 10 young men in their early twenties came from the nearby village of Fort Good Hope every evening to sing, drum, and lead the group in dancing. This experience underlined for many participants the connection between traditional knowledge, cultural practice, and the confident self-esteem that has long been associated with a thorough understanding of, and grounding in, one's traditions.

For the workshop participants involved in other projects, the Dene presentation outlined both the challenges and the dilemmas of the "big picture." One person commented that "It's difficult to learn ecology, language, and social science all at once," and emphasized the necessity of an action plan to take on these tasks one at a time, in achievable segments.

## The Marovo Lagoon Project

The Marovo Lagoon project provided a useful contrast to the Dene presentation — their political contexts were almost opposite. This enabled the workshop participants to distinguish more easily between the broader political implications of some situations and the universal situation of documenting disappearing traditional knowledge in any context.

Unlike the Dene, the people of Marovo Lagoon have clear, recognized title to their land. So far, they have been able to exercise considerable voice in any decisions made by the Solomon Islands government about developments that could affect their resources. Their small scale and relative isolation have protected them from the race to control resources, which has characterized Canadian industry in the Dene homeland. The example of the offshore logging company whose activities damaged the fishing areas of the Marovo clans demonstrated the degree of power the clans were able to exercise when they wished to control unsustainable or incompatible development: they put a stop to the logging.

The residents of Marovo Lagoon have also not been colonized, except by missionaries. As a result, they have retained control of their basic institutions, including the educational system. Their use of resources has remained traditional and their cultural traditions have not been severely disrupted by alcoholism, drug abuse, or consumerism, despite considerable exposure to the West.

The Marovo Lagoon project was initiated by the Marovo elders. At the time, traditional knowledge was becoming rare and poorly understood because of the gradual secularization of Solomon Islands society. Therefore, the principle purpose of the project was to pass traditional knowledge on to the younger generation. The secondary goal was to improve conservation, based on elders' observations of the gradual decline in fish stocks.

In discussion, the two presenters represented different perspectives. One expressed urgent concern about the loss of traditional knowledge; the other expressed optimism about how effectively an educational program could be constructed from documenting the elders' knowledge. Such a program could easily be introduced into the school system. This presenter also felt that there was sufficient time to reverse the loss of environmental knowledge and the decline of fish stocks.

Participants felt that the most exciting contribution of the Marovo presentation was the example it provided of elders initiating and administering a research project, as well as training the researchers about the most important aspects of their tradition. In this instance, the training was cultural and political: the researchers already had advanced degrees, but needed direction from the elders in the goals of the research and the issues that require the most attention.

If the Marovo Lagoon Project was useful for illustrating what might be the best possible scenario for passing on TEK in a neutral political context, the Dene discussion was also useful to the Solomon Islanders, who could foresee the time when their central government would attempt to exert greater control over local governments and encourage developments not in harmony with customary law. In time, they too might come to see TEK as part of their political and cultural armature.

## The Sahel Oral History Project

The Sahel Oral History Project was a sideline of another development project, not the primary objective of SOS Sahel. Considering this, participants felt that the applied focus of the project made it useful in its own right, as well as being useful to the development project. A particulary useful application of TEK, it was felt, would be in constructing the predesertification history of the Sahel, and even the process of desertification itself, as an aid to development planning.

This project thus represented a curious reversal of the others, in being initiated from the outside and intended primarily to serve the objectives of the outside agency. Documenting TEK helped the development agency both in planning well-informed development and in establishing initial contact and trust in the communities. In some cases, it fostered in the communities a sense of ownership and participation in the development project. Participants felt that the oral history project, by demonstrating the usefulness or TEK to development planning initiated by any party, served the overall objectives of all TEK research by sensitizing agencies and the general public to its importance and usefulness. The unfortunate drawback of being a "sideline" project was that there was not enough time to do the desired job.

The project had begun to develop an indexing system for TEK and hoped to learn methods at this workshop to improve its system. This happened to some extent in the discussion and to a greater extent in the wrap-up session on methods.

Brigitte Kone, a native of Mali, played a role in this project roughly parallel to the role played by the Dene researchers in the DCI project. Her presence at the workshop, especially her description of the methods she use to gain the trust of informants and how she rediscovered her roots through the research, provided another example of the value and importance of using indigenous researchers, whether or not the research deals with their actual home communities.

## The Belcher Islands Project

The Belcher Islands presentation provoked discussion on the problems of the very broad definition of TEK, which sometimes leads to vague or conflicting expectations for implementation. Discussion took two directions: the role of outside collaborators in TEK research and the question of what is really new about TEK.

A short debate on the role of outside collaborators divided participants into two camps. One camp felt that there was no place for independent outsiders in TEK research, although they could be useful in implementation. This group felt that outsiders who were not working directly under the direction of the host aboriginal group could jeopardize the exclusive control over the research by the aboriginal group. Such control was deemed necessary to define the research as serving the interests of the host group.

The other camp sympathized with these concerns, but felt that the involvement of independent outsiders could enhance the research process in at least two ways. First, the research would have more credibility in the eyes of government agencies if all the researchers were not working directly for the aboriginal group, but represented an independent and neutral perspective. This would increase the chances of the research having an influence on government, rather than being dismissed as self-serving work by another interest group. Second, outside involvement could add a comparative dimension to the research and help to combine the "inside" and "outside" perspectives. The example from Marovo Lagoon of elders training the outside researchers illustrates that it is possible for outsiders to add their perspectives while working for the aboriginal group.

What is really new in TEK? Is TEK a new frontier? The discussion concluded that the basic information in itself is not new, but that the actors, academic disciplines, and applied focus of the research do represent an important new frontier.

Information on how TEK is acquired, used, and passed on has been documented for at least five decades by cultural ecologists, ethnobotonists, ethnozoologists (subfields of anthropology), and others, usually while studying the adaptation of small-scale, preindustrial societies to their environments. In recent years, such adaptation has begun to be considered as natural resource management. TEK research has included the cultural and polit- ical contexts of management as part of the aboriginal cultural system and sometimes as part of the political system of the nation states where traditional territories lie. Recently, there has been a resurgence of interest in the study of "common property" resources and the community-based management regimes that enable wise and sustainable resource management. This has contributed to the broader context of understanding TEK. In this sense, TEK is neither new as a concept nor as an area of study.

However, current TEK research does involve important new elements. The most obvious is the primary involvement of the host aboriginal community in the direction of the research, including the focus on research leading to application. This element is key, as past anthropological research has not necessar- ily served the aboriginal community by leading to applications; such research often focused strictly on theoretical considera- tions. Without discounting the possible value of theoretical research on TEK, aboriginal peoples see a pressing need for applied and "action" TEK research.

To this can be added the involvement of biologists, other natural scientists, and agency resource managers. Wildlife and fisheries managers are trained to think of hunters and fishers as predators who must be controlled, rather than as human groups operating out of, and controlled by, their own cultural and political systems. As such, their involvement is crucial. It would promote a dialogue between natural and social sciences and further the focus on application.

Studies in TEK are breaking new ground in forcing actors who have traditionally worked in separate spheres to deal with each another. Bridging the natural and social sciences is as difficult as it is important, and it should not be surprising that defining TEK is a problem. The definition is much more comprehensive than conventional anthropological, biological, or academic studies alone can provide.

## Other Presentations

### The Amazon Cultural Centre

The presentation by the Amazon Cultural Centre involved a concept in search of funding rather than an ongoing project. Most of the presentation focused on the political and ecological situation of the Amazon rain forest and the enormous barriers faced by those who wished to document and apply TEK. The discussion revolved mostly around strategies for getting a project started. This lead to related discussions on raising the consciousness in the industrialized countries about the impact of eating less beef, on obtaining funds to document TEK through film, and on finding markets for subsistence products that would help keep traditional knowledge alive and allow people to support themselves by using it.

Many of the political and ecological themes of this presentation echoed the Dene presentation. One important difference was that there is no concept of land title in Brazil unless 50% of the trees are cut and the land is converted to agricultural or livestock production.

## The Comanagement Agreements in Washington State

To situate TEK more clearly in the context of management application, the workshop rapporteur, Evelyn Pinkerton, gave a brief presentation on the fisheries comanagement agreements between the treaty tribes of western Washington State, USA, and the State's natural resource management agencies.

The earliest and most successful agreement was between the tribes and the Washington Department of Fisheries, based on Phase I of the landmark 1974 case, US versus Washington (the Boldt Decision). This case recognized both an allocation right and a management right of the treaty tribes, necessitating cooperation between the tribes and the Washington Department of Fisheries to coordinate management decisions on shared resources. However, translating this court decision into management practice has been a difficult and lengthy process. The most contentious issues was the sharing of knowledge and reaching agreement about what knowledge would form the basis for management decisions.

Before the court decision, Washington State had little data on individual salmon runs that returned to separate tribal rivers. They collected data on overall run size by species in large areas such as North Puget Sound and South Puget Sound. The tribes insisted that knowledge of individual runs to separate tribe rivers was essential for sound management. Otherwise, a fishery on a large run returning to one river might devastate a small run from another river that was passing through a marine area at the same time. Twenty different tribes, whose rights were recognized, each depended on different runs and were determined to protect them.

Over time, the tribes were able to force the State to take their concerns about individual runs seriously and to reorient salmon management toward a watershed perspective. In addition, an information-sharing system was worked out so that both tribes and State had access to the same data. Harvest data was entered on a daily basis into the University of Washington computer and was accessible to all parties for in-season analysis of run size and allocation. All parties also shared escapement and stock assessment data. The tribes, because of their concern for particular watersheds, often applied different analyses to this data than the State. Their different analyses would sometimes lead them to radically different management recommendations.

Resolution of such differences was hampered for the first 10 years after the Boldt Decision by the reluctance of the Washington Department of Fisheries to consider the tribes as legitimate managers. This resistance might have continued indefinitely had not a new governor in 1981 decided to try another route. The governor appointed a new agency head, who eventually replaced five of the top fisheries managers. Finally, a comanagement agreement was negotiated in 1984 and adopted by the court in 1985.

This agreement, called the Puget Sound Salmon Management Plan, laid out the framework and schedule within which the tribes and State would share data and jointly make management decisions. The success of this agreement laid the foundation for subsequent negotiations and agreements. These dealt with an international Pacific salmon treaty, the protection of fisheries habitat, regional planning for the coordination of hatchery production and levels of harvest on different wild and hatchery stocks, the local assessment and planning for reduced levels of nonpoint pollution, and the local planning of equitable water sharing. All these agreements have improved different aspects of fisheries management.

Implementation of the Puget Sound Salmon Management Plan has already led to the protection of biological diversity and to increased run sizes of most salmon species in Puget Sound. For example, the natural chum salmon run of Nooksack River has tripled in size since the early 1970s. Natural runs of pink, chum, and chinook salmon in Puget Sound have approximately doubled in size over the same period.

During discussion of this presentation, some participants wondered if the Puget Sound Salmon Management Plan, requiring the tribes to hire biologists and use Western scientific knowledge and management models, was a "sell-out" of their TEK. Had the tribes accepted too much of the scientific model? Had they formalized their management system too much? Others felt that the legal guarantee of participation was the key element, and that the tribes had a lot of room to use their own knowledge alongside Western knowledge and models. By having the power to define their own priorities and the power to take the Department of Fisheries to court, the tribes could honour their local, holistic perspectives on management issues. Their biologists serve the tribe and can work with elders and other knowledgeable observers of the local watershed ecosystem.

What is important about this example is not how much traditional knowledge has survived in Washington, but what it tells us about how traditional and scientific knowledge can be integrated. The Washington example also highlights the importance of comamagement agreements in protecting the right of indigenous groups to use their own sources and analyses of scientific data. In doing so, it points to the likely future of TEK research.

## *Highlights and Themes*

To draw out some of the highlights and common themes of the presentations, the Marovo Lagoon and the DCI projects were compared along five dimensions. The goal of this comparison was to identify more clearly some of the key issues and common elements in TEK research.

## Tenure

In the Dene situation, there is no clear institutionalized recognition of aboriginal title, although there is some political power to stop, delay, or alter developments, and some preferential harvesting rights (with caribou, for example). In contrast, Marovo Lagoon involves 97% ownership of the land and the power to veto development projects. This factor alone determines an important part of the expectations for, and structure of, TEK research. For example, the Dene have been discussing a comanagement agreement with government, but recent court rulings on aboriginal rights could affect their situation and how they might view TEK. In the Dene situation, TEK can be seen as closely connected with affirmation of land ownership and management rights.

## Defining the Problem

In addition to the simple and obvious problem of the erosion of TEK, related problems affect how TEK research is viewed. For the Dene, a major problem is the rise in consumerism and materialistic expectations in current lifestyles, especially among Dene youth. Alongside a desire to foster continued and revitalized traditional subsistence, the Dene seek a balance between living off the land and meeting cash income needs. In contrast, residents of Marovo Lagoon currently have no major cash needs; their cash income is small and mostly in the service of subsistence activities. If current trends continue, their central problem will be population growth. The ratio of population to resources will probably not permit a sustainable use of resources over the long term.

## Long-Term Strategy

Both the Dene and the people of Marovo Lagoon seek to re-educate their youth about their connection to the land. In Marovo Lagoon, it is a case of reinforcing knowledge that is becoming weaker and creating an awareness of a changing future. In the Dene homeland, it is a case of assisting the most knowledgeable elders in passing on their knowledge to the youth, and assisting the community in evaluating the extent to which they can support themselves off the land without overexploiting it. Learning TEK may also reinforce a self-definition of cultural autonomy through self-support on the land.

### Short-Term Strategy

Both the Dene and the Marovo Lagoon situations share a short-term strategy. They hope to document TEK to preserve the valuable knowledge of the elders. They hope to put TEK into a form that can be fed back to the youth and to develop an educational system that can make TEK meaningful to this youth and meaningful for decision-makers in resource management, in both the aboriginal community and government agencies.

### Methods

The Dene are training their own researchers to work with the elders. In Marovo Lagoon, the elders are training outsiders in how to document TEK.

## Final Discussion

Because of the vastly different contexts, most participants felt that it was difficult to generalize about the research and premature to make recommendations about management systems. In some sense, this amounted to a recognition that it is perhaps more appropriate to take on one issue at a time (such as data management and indexing systems). The workshop explored the full range of issues related to TEK and helped participants to situate their work within this range. Participants learned that they were in very different situations; what they could compare at this point was quite limited.

Tasks suggested as part of future networking included exchanging questionnaires (done by the Dene at this workshop), reviewing the types of collaboration that seem successful, more clearly identifying what type of TEK research is being done (using some of the categories produced in the discussions), and continuing to educate both the public and management agencies about TEK. In countries such as Brazil, where TEK is not recognized, international conferences and film crews should be used to document the use of traditional resources. In all countries, an attempt should be made to develop the marketing of value-added products that represent a more complete use of subsistence goods (such as caribou hides). Finally, to promote public understanding, TEK should be linked to the issue of sustainable resource management. After all, sustainability is part of the very definition of TEK.